'Like this book, fire is a communicator to let people know the right fire for the right place and the right times of the year. Everyone should know about Aboriginal fire knowledge, and keeping the land clean to protect the environment and their homes.' *Uncle Russell Butler, Bandjin and Tagalaka Elder*

'*Fire Country* is without a doubt the most important book I've worked on in my twenty-five-year career as an editor. The knowledge it contains is astounding.' *Tricia Dearborn, editor and author of Autobiochemistry, The Ringing World*

'Given the current dire situation of Australia's bushfires, it is paramount that now, more than ever, the stories in *Fire Country* are heard and enacted upon for the betterment of all Australians, our wildlife and our sustainable ecosystems. Our ancient ways must become our new ways.' *Nova Peris, Olympian, former federal senator, 1997 Young Australian of The Year*

'Biri (fire) holds great spiritual meaning, with many stories, memories and dance being passed down from countless biri practitioners. To have clean water, you need a healthy landscape. To have a healthy landscape, you need biri ... May the Eternal Flame burn forever with *Fire Country.*' *Uncle (Dr) David Dahwurr Hudson, Ewamian and Westen Yalanji Traditional Owner*

'This important book is a story of determination and commitment to restore the knowledge of cultural responsibilities and practices of cultural fire in the Australian landscape. Victor Steffensen offers understandings of Indigenous cultural practices, the relation of people to country, the healing potential of cultural fire, and the way the practices have grown over twenty years.' *Dr Jacqueline Gothe, Associate Professor, School of Design, University of Technology Sydney*

'Victor's work and wisdom is the knowledge our land needs right now. An important reminder of our responsibility to country and the need to respect our Aboriginal knowledge systems, it is essential reading for all Australians.' *Professor Larissa Behrendt, Jumbunna Institute, University of Technology Sydney*

'For anyone interested in understanding ancient Indigenous fire knowledge as a transformative practice for survival. *Fire Country* is the true voice of the land singing out for healing and action at a moment when all life on this planet is under threat. A grassroots visionary, Victor poetically leads with the 'right fire' story for future generations.' *Dr Jason De Santolo, Associate Professor, School of Design, University of Technology Sydney*

'This turns the conventional thinking upside down, a must-read for all of those involved in land management.' *Barry J. Hunter, land management practitioner, Djabugay Aboriginal Corporation*

'In *Fire Country*, Victor Steffensen has written a detailed and elegant account of Aboriginal traditional knowledge that he learnt from the Elders in Cape York. The wisdom of the Elders shines on every page. Of all the explanations of Aboriginal knowledge systems as science, this is the one I would turn to … Even our best scientists acknowledge that we must reinstate Aboriginal environmental knowledge and what was once a continent-wide system of land management, using fire as a friend not an enemy. Victor's book will be a fundamental text for all of us involved in trying to prevent such fire disasters in the future. *Professor Marcia Langton AM, Foundation Chair of Australian Indigenous Studies, University of Melbourne, author of* Welcome to Country

'This is the most potentially game-changing book to emerge in this time of turbulence and transition. It is not a book only about fire. It contains Indigenous knowledge that will work for anyone, from any discipline and any walk of life.' *Tyson Yunkaporta, author of* Sand Talk

FIRE
COUNTRY

HOW INDIGENOUS FIRE MANAGEMENT
COULD HELP SAVE AUSTRALIA

VICTOR STEFFENSEN

Hardie Grant

EXPLORE

Published in 2020 by Hardie Grant Explore, a division of Hardie Grant Publishing

Hardie Grant Explore (Melbourne)
Wurundjeri Country
Building 1, 658 Church Street
Richmond, Victoria 3121

Hardie Grant Explore (Sydney)
Gadigal Country
Level 7, 45 Jones Street
Ultimo, NSW 2007

www.hardiegrant.com/au/explore

A catalogue record for this
book is available from the
National Library of Australia

Hardie Grant acknowledges the Traditional Owners of the Country on which we work, the
Wurundjeri People of the Kulin Nation and the Gadigal People of the Eora Nation, and
recognises their continuing connection to land, waters and culture. We pay our respects to
their Elders past and present.

Fire Country
ISBN 9781741177268

10 9 8

Publisher
Melissa Kayser
Editor
Tricia Dearborn
Editorial Assistant
Jessica Smith
Proofreader
Rosanna Dutson
Prepress
Splitting Image Colour Studio

All images are © Victor Steffensen, except for last image in the colour insert which is
© Alasdair McDonald
Cover design by Tristan Schultz
Typeset in Minion Pro 11pt by Mike Kuszla
Printed in Australia by Griffin Press, an Accredited ISO AS/NZS 14001
Environmental Management System printer

This book is dedicated to all of the young and upcoming generations to be the turning point of reconnecting humanity with land and culture again.

Aboriginal and Torres Strait Islander readers are advised that this book may contain images and names of people who have died.

Contents

Introduction

From a young age I grew up knowing very little about my mother's family and our Aboriginal heritage. I was always curious to know about that side of the family and keen to learn more about culture. Living in Australia means living on Aboriginal land, so I had strong reasons to understand my own connection. Every time I asked my mum questions she would tell me that my grandmother never talked about it. I've heard many Elders say that it brings too much pain and bad memories for most Aboriginal people from those generations. Many people were separated from their families, given different names and then sent to different parts of the country.

This also happened to my Nan's family around the 1920s in a town called Croydon in the Gulf of Carpentaria. It happened to many of the Tagalaka people and their country. In those times, most Aboriginal people were sent away to missions or sent to unpaid work for the new establishments. As in many places the language was lost, their lands taken, leaving many people deprived of their culture, some not even knowing who they are related to. The only thing I have recorded from those days are some old police documents. Nan didn't even get a last name when she was born, so with no birth certificate her name was just Ada until she was to be married. She had been separated from her brothers. They never really saw each other again after that. One was sent to Palm Island and the other was sent to work on cattle stations.

Nana Ada was first sent to look after a white cattle-farming family.

She would cook, serve, clean, and be a housemaid for them. Mum used to tell me that she had to wipe the seats down before the privileged would sit in them. As I listened to the few stories my mother could tell me, I tried to imagine what it would have been like for my Elders in that time. My grandmother died when I was only five years old, so I never got to sit down to listen to her stories. If only I could have a conversation with her now – so many questions to try and enlighten me on what was lost in the past.

Like many places in Australia at that time, the tribes were hit hard by genocide. It is a similar story among so many clan groups abroad, and each suffered in similar way because of it. Some were lucky enough to retain their language and connection to country, and some retained very little at all. Some were able to keep their original features and others became a mixed race with other nations. All proud to be Aboriginal just the same. At one stage it was part of the government's plan to breed the black out of the Aboriginal race. Trying hard to erase the blood of the people, and erase their place from the land.

Not all white fellas were bad in any era or time, but we can't forget the terrible stories from those old days, the cruel deeds that did happen. It is beyond anyone's mind to understand the damage that has been done to the people and the environment up until this day, and our history is a part of that. The country and people are still suffering in so many places across the globe. Here in Australia the land is suffering more than ever before. The genocide that was cast upon the people is still affecting the country today. So before I talk about the story of bringing back the good fire, I want to acknowledge my family, my mentors, and the love for culture and country as my inspiration to write this book. A contribution to help heal the wounds of the past so they don't become problems for our children's future.

This story is just one Aboriginal fire story of many across Australia that are calling people back to country to put the right fire back onto the land. The fire is just the beginning of understanding the important journey ahead for us all.

Part one

Finding the old people

Chapter 1
Finding the old people

Through my childhood I was always interested in learning whatever I could about culture and the bush. I never grew up on country linked to my heritage; instead, my hometown was a little village in the rainforest called Kuranda, the home of the Djabugay people. There were people from other clan groups from all over living there too, from the earlier mission days. A large hippie population moved into town in the late sixties and seventies and set up camp too. There are still some of the old-school ones living there, cruising around. We all went to school barefoot; even when we played sport we didn't wear shoes.

I was lucky to grow up in that little rainforest town back then – there was lots of village talent to inspire. A free-living place with plenty of live music, fresh food markets, and far-out characters. Just about everyone could play the guitar and we would have long nights down the river jamming by the fire. I loved playing music, and getting into drama, as artistic inspiration was all around me. The best thing about Kuranda in those days was the Barron River. Everyone loved spending time along the sandy riverbanks every day. Always going fishing and camping with my good brothers under the stars. Telling hairy-man stories as we tried to sleep on the cold sand, listening for him walking around through the night. I wanted to learn more about culture, and throughout my childhood I picked up whatever I could from my own surroundings.

My early school days in Kuranda are golden memories that always make me smile. But high school wasn't all that fun for me. That's when the rules came in to start wearing shoes. There wasn't anything at school that suited my personal interests, except drama class, in the first couple of years. Then the only thing that kept me at high school after that was basketball. We played every morning and afternoon, on the school team and in our hometown team, as the Kuranda Cassowaries. I grew to love playing the game because my friends were into it too. Every day I would jump the backyard fence and run down to the outdoor basketball court. At the end of the day most of the young men met up to play amazing touch footy games on the school oval.

As a kid, the hardest thing about growing up was understanding my Aboriginality as a mixed-raced person. There are a few different blood lines running through our particular family tree, like many Aboriginal people have now. German, English, Dad used to say he had Viking blood too, but I was taught by my mother to be respectful of them all. Kids in those days could be cruel and they questioned my identity on many occasions when I shared my Aboriginal heritage. But I had the ability to hang around and be comfortable with both the Aboriginal kids and the white kids, which allowed me to hear trash talk on both sides. No matter who I heard it from, it always hurt when I heard racist remarks. I would go home confused and tell my mum what some kids would say at school about Aboriginal people. She would respond by saying, 'Don't you ever forget that you have Aboriginal blood too. You tell them that and don't worry about what anybody says.'

It always made me feel better when she told me that, but I knew there was something missing. I didn't know enough about Aboriginal culture and I had no one to teach me what I wanted to know. It was a huge void in my life, a gap I wanted to fill. I certainly didn't know anything about Aboriginal fire knowledge as a kid; they didn't teach it at school and I lived in the rainforest. But I did have a fascination with fire, that was for sure. I loved making camp fires down the river and flicking matches around, watching them ignite as they flew through the air. I guess I was more of a fire bug than anything else, but what do you expect from a little kid?

I do remember my very first fire, though, and it certainly is one of the fires that I remember the most. I was about eight years old when I grabbed a packet of Redheads matches and went to play in the backyard. I ended up exploring the big banana patch that was growing right behind our chicken pen at the time. I stood in the middle of the banana patch, crunching on a huge pile of dead leaves. It was too good an opportunity to refuse. It was like those dead leaves were begging me to strike a match and burn them to a cinder. That is exactly what I did – I struck the match and the fire started instantly, burning the dry banana leaves to a point where I realised it was out of control.

The flames went wild and started to flame up over the chicken pen, which housed at least twenty or more fowls that fed our family. The flames rose up and engulfed the banana trees that my dad prized so much. I realised that I was about to burn down the chicken pen and that I was in big trouble. I began to panic and ran up to the house to find some way to put out the fire. My older sister was the only person I could find and she yelled out, 'You're in trouble. Quick, grab the hose!' By now the flames were starting to rise above the roof of the chicken coop and all I could think about was the hiding I was going to get from my father. My sister ran over to turn the tap on as I grabbed the hose and dashed towards the chicken pen as fast as I could.

I ran with the hose in hand at full speed towards the crime scene, then I ran out of hose, which jerked me up in the air to land flat on my back. The hose was way too short to reach the pen. All I could do was sit there and watch the flames as they engulfed the chicken coop. Luckily, Dad came to the rescue and started to put the fire out with buckets of water. He saved our chickens from being roasted alive, but the worst was yet to come. I sat there and waited for him to come over and give me the good old-fashioned hiding. That would have to be the worst trouble I have ever gotten into for lighting a fire. Little did I know that I was going to light a lot more fires in my lifetime.

By the age of seventeen I had left my home and school to head out into the big wide world. I wanted to find a way to become a ranger and be out in the bush. The only option I had came through my Aboriginal liaison officer at school. Unexpectedly, he had set me up for special entry into Canberra University to study cultural heritage. I needed a special entry because I didn't do too well with my senior school marks, except for cooking classes. The bizarre side of taking that uni course was that I would have to live in Canberra, the last of all places you would expect to see a North Queensland boy. Before long, I got accepted and found myself at Canberra University.

On campus I was living with other Indigenous students from around the country. I soon learnt that the only important things were hot food and keeping warm. All the other Indigenous students became family and we would look after each other. It was more about survival for us at that age, chucking in for food and taking turns at cooking meals. But when it came down to study I did try hard. One of the classes I had to do was English. It was extremely difficult and, with all due respect, not my cuppa tea. I didn't see how it was relevant to what I was wanting to learn at the time. So between that and the freezing cold weather, I only lasted a long three months before I went back home. Once one of us left to go home, most of the others followed and went back to their hometowns soon after. University may have been the wrong choice for me at that time, but it was a good short-lived memory, and at least I tried.

By mid-1991, I was home again in the sunny warm north, on the case of working out what to do next. Dad was hounding me to get a job and start doing something with my life. I didn't have a clue what to do at the time; I'd only just turned eighteen. The next best thing that came along was an invite from some Kuranda friends to go fishing out bush, up north to a little town called Laura in the lower region of Cape York. That sounded like a good opportunity, so I packed a swag and a fishing line, and jumped in the car with the rest of them. Little did I know that day was a one-way ticket to the bush and the beginning of my pathway in life.

We drove the long rough dusty road, listening to music and laughing along the way. I had no idea where we were going, or what to expect. When we arrived at Laura, I saw that it was a very small country town with a population of about a hundred people – a bit more when you included the pastoral residents on the outskirts. It was a town with the basics: a tiny school, a general store, a cafe, police station, clinic, and the old Quinkan Hotel.

One of the friends I was travelling with knew the people of the community pretty well and was also related to some. He wasn't only going fishing, but also looking for a job there. The town had a small Aboriginal corporation that ran a community development employment program, or CDEP. We were welcomed into the community and directed to a place where we could camp. It was good to be with someone who knew everyone, because I was a total stranger. Once we were settled in, I started to check out the Laura scene.

Most people were sitting out the front of the houses in the main street, yarning under the mango trees. I met a few people who came over to say hello; it was a fairly friendly environment. As I continued to look around I could see two old men from a distance, sitting with their families. Their names were George Musgrave and Tommy George. I was told that they were brothers, and were among the most respected and knowledgeable men in the area. I was instantly intrigued by their status and wanted to learn more about them. As I peered over at them I could see that they were watching me. Even when they weren't looking at me, it felt like they were watching me. They had a really strong presence that I was drawn to, but it made me nervous to think of approaching them.

I continued listening to my friends talking about the possibility of getting a job here. One of them suggested that I should ask for a job too, which involved asking the Elders and the local chairman of the community. I wasn't too sure about that; I wanted to go fishing first. Before long, a Toyota ute rolled up and we were told to jump in the back. A couple of the locals were taking us out to a waterhole to try to catch some barramundi.

Away we went, over dirt roads through the bush, standing up on the back of the Toyota tray. It felt so good being out bush, hunting and being free, without a care in the world. We fished all day and while we didn't really get much fish, we were happy being out on the land, enjoying the experience. As the day ended we got back into our positions on the Toyota and started on our way back to the community. I was standing on the back of the ute with my eyes combing the bushlands, in awe of the freedom. It was at that moment I thought to myself that being in the bush was where I wanted to be.

The next day my travelling friends were getting serious about signing up for jobs on CDEP. Fred Coleman, the chairman of the organisation, gave them approval, which made them happy. Then they turned to me and asked again if I wanted a job. I said yes, Mr Coleman gave his approval and soon enough I was signing on to join the local community workforce. I had my first job out in the big wide world. It was a work-for-the-dole program, but it was still a job to me. I was totally rapt: I went fishing and hooked a job in a little bush town.

The only problem was where I was going to live. There was already not enough housing to accommodate everyone. For a population of over a hundred people there were only eight houses for the Aboriginal community to use. One house was haunted and no one wanted to live in that one. There was a ghost of a woman with a white dress and long black hair that lived there. They called it the number eight house, and it stood mysterious and empty at the end of the street. So that left seven dwellings to house the population.

The next house I inspected only had one man living in it. That man was one of the two elderly brothers, old man Tommy George, or TG for short. He was sitting there, perched up on his front porch, smoking his pipe. He was watching every move going on in the dusty main street. The reason no one lived with him is because no one in the community could. It was his house and it was under his rules: no alcohol, don't touch his stuff, and no making a nuisance of yourself. If they broke his rules, he would literally kick their arses out onto the street. That left six houses.

The next house belonged to the older brother, George Musgrave (Poppy). Poppy was living in his house with his family, so that left five houses which were pretty full with the remaining families. As I stood there thinking about where I was going to camp I heard a gravelly voice call out to me, 'Hey boy'. It was old man TG, sitting on his front porch, giving a hand signal for me to come over. I walked over, a little nervous, and stood in front of him. He was puffing on an old cow horn he'd made into a pipe and sipping on a big billy tin full of tea. I mean, it wasn't a cup he was drinking out of, but an actual large billy tin. He said, 'You looking for a place to stay?' I gave him a nod and he went on to say, 'Well, you can stay with me. This is my house.'

I gave him a big smile in appreciation. 'You can go inside and choose one of the spare rooms', he said. I thanked him and then slowly walked into the house. I walked along the wooden floors and down the hallway to find an empty room to lay my swag. From that day on I was living with old man TG, and I started feeling comfortable quickly. Just the two of us, sharing a three-bedroom house all to ourselves. I was on my best behaviour and started helping him around the house straight away. Within no time I was cooking a good feed and making tea for us both while he told me endless stories. There was no escape once he started telling stories, he would go on for hours most times.

The day after I moved in I was properly introduced to his older brother, Poppy. He was sitting in the front yard with his family, interacting with the rest of the community on the main street. I was curious to meet the respected Elder, so old TG got his attention for my introduction. 'Brother, this boy here is gonna stay with me.' Poppy didn't look over yet. 'Aw, yeah', he said slowly, acknowledging his brother. I said hello and he gave me a quick glance and said hello back. He then went on with what he was doing, without any further conversation. Old TG went on to tell Poppy that I had a job in the community and that I lived in his house. 'Aw, yeah, that's good', Poppy replied, and that was the end of our first meeting. It took a little longer for me to get to know Poppy, I had to earn his respect.

Sitting back on the porch that afternoon, like many, with old man TG, I soon learnt that there was never a dull moment in little old Laura town. There was something happening every day in the main street. You didn't need a television – there was plenty of action going on. People were coming and going all the time. Like any small town there was happiness, sadness, dramas and endless laughter that filled the little street on most days. There were a few drinks being had among some, which was the way it was in those times. But everyone was family, and I soon warmed to the town's community life.

Besides the everyday social side of the place, the best part was going to work on my new job. The Elders would go to work with us too, doing all sorts of jobs around the place. They were more or less the bosses of the whole community and workforce at that time. If you stepped out of line, you were in big trouble. It was working with them on country that allowed me to get to know them better. I worked hard with the crew and a few weeks later I was upgraded to a new job as community ranger. I still got paid the same amount of money as everyone else on four days a week, except they gave me a ranger uniform. Old TG was the head ranger and he told everyone that he was the boss. He had his uniform on all the time; he lived and breathed being a ranger and looking after country. He was so happy about my recruitment and the fact that I was now officially working under him. From that day on I went on countless adventures with them old people.

Every day we would go out bush, hunting, fishing, or collecting materials to make medicines or artefacts like woomeras (spear-throwers). We were often bringing the younger kids along or sometimes going out on our own. Those two old people, old man TG and Poppy, took me under their wing and shared their world with me. Being with them on country made me feel grateful for each and every day. The best part was being out on country most of the time, completely free from any cares. If I wasn't working then I was listening and learning about animals, plants, places or stories. We didn't just talk about it – we would eat bush tucker, craft wood into an artefact, or make medicine, just as the old people did in the old days.

I told the Elders that my grandmother came from the Tagalaka people in Croydon. They told me a story about when they were in their early twenties – they had worked over in Croydon doing cattle on one occasion. It would have been around the mid-1940s when they were over there. Old TG told me that they met an old Tagalaka man there who could also speak Kuku-Thaypan. Even though the clan groups were so far apart, they could speak each other's language. I was interested to hear such a story and the language connections all the clan groups would've had before settlement. They taught me parts of the Awu-Laya language, refreshing their memories as they spoke in their native tongue.

It was an honour to learn from them, but it didn't come without many challenges along the way. You have to develop trust, not just with the old people, but the whole community. It took some time before the old people really started to teach me things. They also found me useful to help them out too around other life matters. The main thing they wanted was to practise culture and get back onto their country. They wanted to apply their knowledge back onto the land, the fire, the water, looking after the story places. But most of all they wanted their younger ones to learn the language and get back onto country. It was vital because the two men were the last of the Awu-Laya Elders who knew the traditional knowledge and stories of that country. They wanted the young ones to inherit the knowledge and take over their roles as leading Elders.

That proved to be challenging for them due to modern town life and the influences that came with it. The old men gave up drinking before I met them, they had finished with those days. There were many good yarns had with other Elders enjoying a brew, though. Some old characters I sat with around the camp fire were hard, old cattle men. After the conversations they would lie out on the ground and sleep with no swag at all under the stars.

Old man TG told me that he came from the days where only hard-working men were allowed to have a drink. So on occasion, after work, he would tell me to go sit with everyone and join the party. I would often contribute by bringing my six-string guitar and sing all kinds of old songs with everyone. There was never any problem getting people to sing and dance under the old shady mango trees.

Old man TG loved music, and was always happy when I pulled out the old guitar for a strum. I would play for him all the time and he loved it so much. He could play a bit as well and would pluck the strings now and then. His favourite song was 'You Are My Sunshine', so we would play that one quite often. You had to create your own fun, so music became a big part of our down time. I began teaching the drums to a young boy named Trevor. He lived with me and old TG through periods of his childhood, from a young age. I taught him how to play with two sticks on some empty boxes and saucepans. I played songs on the guitar, and he would bash sticks on whatever we could find. Together we would make music and entertained ourselves for hours.

We began to find some rhythm, so I saved up and got an old set of second-hand drums, an amp and a microphone. We didn't have a mic stand but we used a broom handle, a chair, and some sticky tape. We started a two-man band for the Laura community and old man TG was the manager. It was his band and he called it the Laura Quinkan Country Band. We would play all night down at the local Quinkan Hotel almost every weekend. Sometimes the community would keep us playing until three in the morning, until the pub owner walks over and shuts down the main power. People danced and cheered; the whole community was so happy. We were a two-man juke box and everyone appreciated the different genres we could play: rock'n'roll, country, reggae, and even a love song here and there. Some of the punters would cry with joy and shake a leg to some tunes. Whenever Trevor played 'Wipe Out' on the drums he would make all of his Aunties cry. 'That's my son,' they would say, bursting into tears with pride. It was so much fun, jamming to a dancing community all night. It was an amazing time. Everyone was together as one – white and black, kids and adults. Life was good back then in little old Laura town.

But partying up was something I always put last on the list when it came to country and culture. I always put the old people and country first, every time, no exceptions. Every time we went bush, we would try and take the grandchildren with us, especially Dale and Lewis Musgrave. They were the two eldest grandsons of Poppy and TG. They would come out with us on trips all over the country. Poppy's youngest daughter, Eleanor, would also come along, and other younger children like Trevor, and their families. The old people were always throwing the kids in the tray of the Toyota to take them out on country. They would constantly tell the younger ones that they would take over from them one day, and they always made sure to bring them along with us whenever possible.

It wasn't long before the old fellas started talking about going down to the local schoolhouse to teach the kids. They started teaching the

Awu-Laya language and cultural lessons at the local school. We did bush tucker walks, dance, made bush humpies, started fire, and sang songs in language.

We had a regular gig at the school once a week for an hour in the afternoon. Them old people were so proud that they would tell the whole town about their little language program. I don't think we would've missed one lesson, as it was high on our agenda. I even had my own two children going to the school as well. I was raising a family through all of this too, which made things even better. Life really was good in little old Laura town.

Chapter 2
Hiding in the mailbags

George Musgrave and Tommy George were Awu-Laya men, Kuku-Thaypan people. Their wives and in-laws were traditionally from Laura, but they all lived on and looked after their wives' country all the same. They were living within their traditional clan kinship system that the people of that region have kept to for thousands of years. George and Tommy were born on their country and they would take me to their birthplaces to show me. Old TG was always proud to show me where he was born, under a tree at Eighteen Mile Lagoon. Poppy was the oldest and he would have been born around 1920 at Musgrave Station. He was roughly eight years older than TG.

Both of them grew up on country with their families, who were still living close to the traditional lifestyle. In those days, they were among the few left living who didn't get taken away by the police. All the children would get taken away, but the brothers managed to avoid that situation. The reason they managed to avoid capture was a white station owner by the name of Frederick Shepard. Fred Shepard bought and owned Musgrave Station and a large parcel of land that took up most of Awu-Laya country. George and Tommy's family stayed and became workers for the cattle owner, so Frederick had young George and Tommy working for him from a young age.

Fred didn't want the police to take the boys so he hid them in the mailbags every time the police came around. In those days the people were still using horses, as the roads were originally built for wagons. The

Austin Seven automobiles were travelling up the Cape for the first time around 1928, so there weren't that many cars. The old men would tell the story of them both hiding in the storeroom, tucked away in the bags, sitting quiet as they heard the police talking down below. 'You haven't got any black kids here have you?' the police would say. Old Fred Shepard would say no, he didn't have any Aboriginal kids around the place.

When the police overstayed their welcome at times, Fred would sneak some food and water in for the boys. The old fellas would sometimes stay in those bags overnight. They had to stay there until it was safe to come out. There were also times where they had escaped the police other ways while out in the bush, away from the homestead. They had seen their countrymen of similar ages get caught by the police, some never seen again. A few of the ones taken came back later in life at an old age. But sadly they would come back not knowing their language or their country. They told me stories of how they saw men and women being walked for miles with chains around their necks, whip marks were no stranger, and some unable to continue the torturous walk. They were growing up in some hard times for Aboriginal people.

The brothers were barely in their teenage years when they became hard-working cattlemen. In time they ended up mustering cattle and herding them to the saleyards on horseback, over five hundred kilometres away. Some trips would take many weeks to herd hundreds of heads all the way to the nearest sale yards in Mareeba. They would sleep in the rain with blankets, get up at the crack of dawn, and in those days they even shoed some of the cattle. Crossing the cattle through raging crocodile-infested rivers and living life like the wild west. They were Aboriginal cattlemen and they were as tough as nails.

They had a reputation for being among the better fighters in the area too. Many men fell from the strike of their taipan fists in occasional conflicts brewed throughout their stories. Those rougher days moulded them into amazing, knowledgeable, hard men of the Cape.

On the cultural side of their story, they got to stay on country and learn from the Elders of that time. They got to learn their language and were taught about the bush from the Elders' traditional ways. They knew the traditional lore of their homelands and all the stories within the landscape. They knew how to look after the land, including the use of traditional fire management practices. They were knowledge holders from the last peoples that were living traditionally on country.

If it wasn't for old Fred Shepard hiding those boys from the police, they would have been taken from country as well. They would have been sent to missions and may never have learnt as much knowledge as they did. The old fellas had a lot of respect for old Fred Shepard and they thought of him like a father. They would refer to him as old Dad and from that they had respect for the whole Shepard family. They even considered Fred's sons, who still live on the cattle properties today, to be brothers. But none of Fred's children really knew how much knowledge George and Tommy had of their culture and land. I guess that Aboriginal knowledge wasn't valued as much in those days – it was all working cattle for the property owners and that was just the way it was.

The old fellas ended up getting married as they got older and lived in Laura with their wives. Fred Shepard died in 1952 and George and Tommy never got to go to the funeral.

I was moved by the relationship they had with that man and I could still see they were disappointed by not going to his funeral. I ended up asking the old fellas if they wanted to visit his grave in Mareeba. They said yes, and asked me to find out where old Dad Fred Shepard was laid to rest. I ended up walking around the old Mareeba cemeteries for a couple of days until I finally found the old man. There he was: Frederick Shepard, died 1952. I went back to Laura to pick up the two old men and then drove them back down to visit the cemetery. They stood at the foot of Fred's grave with their hats off, respecting the resting place of that man. They were seeing his grave for the first time, forty-five years later, and they were truly thankful. I was thankful too, otherwise we would not have been standing together there that day and I wouldn't be telling you this story.

Part two

_____

The fire

Chapter 3
The fire

I will never forget the day that Poppy lit the first fire on country in front of me.

We were standing in the middle of a small community of boxwood trees about twenty kilometres out of old Laura town. The ecosystem was only as big as a couple of basketball courts and was surrounded by a small creek and stringybark country. The grass was quite thick, dead and dry, and we were standing in it up to our knees. 'I'm gonna light the grass now, like the old people used to do', Poppy said loudly and proudly. He walked over to the stringybark country and ripped off a long piece of bark from the closest tree.

'You look now.' He teased one end of the long piece of bark, lit it up and then walked through the boxwood patch in a repetitive, figure eight type movement. He was almost skipping as he dragged the bark along, making the fire follow him around. I watched him dancing through the flames like some kind of fire spirit sprinkling magic dust onto the land. I watched the fire go higher and the smoke fill the space around him until I couldn't see him anymore. There was nothing but fire in front of me, but it was only seconds before it started to calm down. Then he reappeared in the middle of the fire, walking over the flames with his bare feet, giving me the biggest smile.

The fire soon trickled out, burning a perfect circle that outlined that little patch of boxwood country. I knew he was making fun and showing off in his humble way. 'The old people use to burn the country all the time,' he said, ending with his cheeky high-pitched laugh, which echoed through the trees. It was from that point that we started to focus more on fire and burning the country the old, traditional way.

Poppy was the main man for the fire, his understanding of fire and the country was a special gift. He made sure to teach me well at every opportunity we had together. From place to place, both old men would stop and tell the fire stories for each different landscape. They would talk about the right time to burn, how all the animals fitted in, what plants lived where, and the types of soils.

Trip after trip involved camping, fishing, hunting, and learning fire management lessons along the way. The only problem was we were not free to practise fire in many places. Laura was surrounded by cattle properties and national parks, and there was no talk of Indigenous fire at the time. The only fires were in the late, drier times of the year from pastoralist and national park fires. Poppy and our ranger crew would light small fires around the Aboriginal reserve from time to time, but there were no fire programs at all back then.

But that never stopped us from learning about fire through the indicators on country. You can learn so much about fire on country, even if you don't have a fire burning. You have to know how to read the country and learn the knowledge before you can light a fire.

One day a national park ranger came driving into town, asking if we wanted a job burning country with them. He said he needed a few fellas for a couple of weeks to do the fire management work on the national park. Everyone got along well with the local head ranger there at the time, which was why he asked us. I put my hand up for the job, I was keen to go on one of their burns. The old people didn't want to go, so it was just me, another Aboriginal ranger and a couple of other Traditional Owners from Hope Vale. We packed our swags and away we went to stay out on Lakefield National Park (now called Rinyirru (Lakefield) National Park).

There were two park rangers that gave us a short briefing on what we were going to do. Back then there wasn't much in the way of safety talks or training preparations. We ended up riding on the back of the ranger utes just dressed in our everyday clothes. Each of the vehicles had a slip-on firefighting unit, drip torches, and a flamethrower connected to a drum of fuel. We were told to operate the equipment in the back tray while the rangers were in the air-conditioned cabins. We were off to go and burn some country and it felt like we were really going to conduct an army exercise. It was all to be done to plan and we were there to do what they told us to do.

It was around late October and the landscape was hot, dry and loaded with grassy fuel. Just one match would see the whole place go up in flames. The rangers spread maps across the bonnet of the truck and started pointing their fingers at their plan of attack. 'We are going to burn this side of the road, but not that side', they instructed. Their burn zones were broken up by roads and fences instead of reading the country and burning the right place like the old people do. I was told to sit on the back of the ute with the flamethrower and prepare to take aim. When you pressed the trigger it would squirt a constant stream of fire to about four to five metres. The head ranger then drove along the road while I was told to constantly hold the trigger to leave a line of fire all the way along. The other guys were spraying hoses, using water to create a firebreak. As we were driving along I could see the whole country going up into flames behind us.

Flames started jumping roads and one of the other rangers came driving over in a panic, shouting at us. 'The fire got away!' We had a few heated moments that day, where the fire escaped their burn zone and we had to put it out. I was clinging on the back of the ute holding a fire hose while the ute flew off-road across the rough country. I remember walls of flame almost fifteen feet high raging along at some times. They would just drive straight through the flames in their diesel trucks, leaving us exposed to put them out. We were pouring water on ourselves more than the fire because we were surrounded by licking flames. Straight into the heart of the beast. But as stupid as it all sounds, we did end up controlling all of the fires. We controlled every one of them, but in no way did I feel good about it.

I wondered, 'Why in the hell am I here?' I could see that the rangers didn't know what they were doing. It's not really their fault, that was just the way they knew how in those times. That was the day I decided to avoid any flamethrower or drip torch to use for burning country. They can put too much fire into the landscape, making the fire fuel itself even more. That fire must have torched hundreds of acres that day. Speeding along in a four-wheel drive for kilometres spraying fire everywhere. I was only about nineteen years old at the time and I knew that I would never do that kind of burning again.

When I got back home and told the old people about my adventures, they shook their heads in a concerned way. They already knew too, because they could see the massive plumes of black smoke in the distance. They would complain about national parks often, especially old TG. I would listen to him all the time at home, grumbling about them. 'Those bloody national park rangers, they should be learning from us.'

Because we weren't doing any burns outside of Aboriginal lands at the time, we would stop and look at burns the cattle properties and national parks had done. The old men would tell me to stop the car when we came across any burnt country. They would then explain why the fires were wrong and point out the indicators. In many cases all the country was burnt black, sometimes scorched to nothing for as far as the eye could see. In most cases the trees were scorched, and the canopies completely destroyed. The old people were always pointing it out, complaining all the time with frustration on the boil. What they were seeing was not up to the standards of caring for country through Aboriginal fire knowledge.

The Western fire regimes are based on hazard reduction and they don't see the layers of cultural and environmental connections that make up Aboriginal fire knowledge, which is based on all elements of nature living in harmony with one another. This misinformation about the difference between cultural burning and harzard reduction or back burning was becoming clearer and clearer every time the old people stopped to talk about fire on country.

But it wasn't just the burnt country the old people would stop to look at. They would also do assessments on the country that hadn't had fire in many years. Much of the country we were travelling through was thick with weeds and a mass of dead vegetation for the understory. The old men would comment on how the land was healthy and clean when they were younger. The country is suffering because no one knows how to look after the fire anymore. The more they opened up my eyes to it, the more saddened I became about the state it was in. Here were two of the most knowledgeable men in the region on their own country, and they couldn't do anything about it.

Chapter 4
Starting the fire

A couple of years later the old men had some rights to their own country handed back through native title. It was one of the good things that the local land councils were doing for the communities of Cape York and other communities in the north. There was a ceremony and specific agreements in the form of a document for the families to sign. The agreement acknowledged that they could access their land and do certain activities under their cultural rights. It was a special time and the Elders were so excited to have parts of their homelands handed back to them. They still had to ask the neighbouring station owners for permission and the old fellas always respected that. They also had to go by the rules of national parks and the government, who arranged the agreements on what the Elders could do and couldn't do on their own land.

They couldn't live permanently on their land and there was no support in getting fire, water, or any other form of their own management happening. It was more like a pass to go backstage but you could never be in the band. It wasn't what I would call handing the country back to the owners, but they could go back onto their country all the same. In reality the old people knew it was their country through and through, regardless of the impending Western laws. But the main thing was they had an exciting opportunity, because from that day on the old men were granted the freedom to access their own country.

Before long we were once again driving over old overgrown wagon roads that weaved through their homeland. The old men started reviving traditional knowledge of their waterholes, sacred places and birthplaces. We also went to places where people died and were buried in the same spot. No funerals or death certificates for people in those old days. Endless stories of hardship from the past just poured out of these old people. We would go off the road completely, dodging trees and going through gullies to find places. I always had Poppy's finger as my GPS, sitting up on the dash pointing the way through the rugged bush.

The old men knew where they were going, but they couldn't recognise some of their country from tons of old dead grass and weeds. In most places it was higher than the bonnet of the four-wheel drive. They couldn't recognise landmarks, which made it harder for them to find many important places. In a couple of cases we didn't find the sacred places at all. Some areas they hadn't been able to visit for many years because of the lack of access previously. The Elders complained continuously about the state of the country and were heartbroken. Their land had become sick in many places and they pointed their finger at bad fire management.

Every time we drove through the country, the old people kept saying that it was sick. They would say, 'Oh, look at our country, the grass, we need to burn it.' Then they would wail a long 'Ooooooowwwww', in sorrow for their home and ancestors. I'd say to them in return, 'Burn it, old man.' But they would say, 'No, we have to ask the boss man first.' I referred to the boss men as the three Ps: the police, parks and wildlife, and the pastoralists. The three Ps of power that seem to be the obstacles for cultural revival in our case. It was programmed in old people's minds to have the white fella in charge of everything they did.

They grew up their whole lives having the white fella as the boss man, and so that was how it was for them old people. For me it was harder to accept, coming from my generation. It reminded me of my grandmother and her experiences and the loss of information. If we keep listening to the boss man, we will lose more Elders and knowledge to the grave. I didn't want to see that happen with Poppy and old TG. The more I thought about it the more I wanted to do something to free these old people's imprisoned minds. On and on we went. Every time we drove over the land they would complain on the state of the country, and every time I would say, 'Burn it.' Over time they would start to get a little angry at me pushing them to light the fire. Especially old man TG. 'No, you can't, you gotta ask the boss.' I explained a few times that we had already asked the boss and they wouldn't let us burn the country. The boss men might've made it clear that fire was out of the question for us, but I wasn't going to give up.

I mentioned how important it was to the younger generations, to take care of the country in the future. That we done lots of work with the filming and recording (which I talk about later in this chapter), and that we could show the boss to make him understand. Eventually I could see that Poppy was starting to come around to the idea.

Then one day we went camping for a couple of days at a place called Gno-Coom, or Saxby Waterhole. We had left camp for the day to take a trip around the landscape to visit other special places. It was another one of our usual adventures, driving along the rugged track with the two old men grumbling in my ear about the dry choked-up country. As usual I responded, 'Burn it, old fella. Light it up.' This time Poppy answered 'Alright, pull up.' For the first two seconds those words didn't register, but within the next second after that I stepped hard on the brake in disbelief.

As the vehicle quickly came to a halt Poppy grabbed old TG's lighter, jumped out of the truck and shuffled swiftly over to the dead grass to light it up. Then he quickly jumped back into the truck and gave me the signal to keep driving with his GPS finger pointing in direction. He didn't want to hang around to watch the fire, he knew it wouldn't get out of control and cause damage. As we drove on there was a short silence and then Poppy started explaining what he had just done. He pointed out that the fire would only burn where all the boxwood and gum trees were. He said that it would be good for the country, clean all the old grass away and thin out the invasive tea-tree. After his comforting, wise and logical explanation, the uncomfortable dead silence broke out once more as we drove on to our camp.

I could feel the nervous energy running through all three of us like an electric charge. We knew that we would get into trouble for lighting that fire, but at the same time we were empowered to have done so. I could almost hear all of our hearts beating as my sweating hands gripped the steering wheel. It felt like we were little children going home to face the punishment of our parents after getting up to mischief. I had never experienced these two strong, legendary men give off this kind of energy before.

Still in silence we kept on driving to our camp, which was about ten minutes away from the burn. As our camp came into sight we could also see a four-wheel drive parked right next to our swags. It was the station owners standing there, watching us as we approached. All I could think to myself was 'Oh shit.' Then TG gave out a long 'Ohhh nooo' as he pulled his smoking pipe out of his mouth in disbelief. Poppy gave a low groan and then that timeless deadly silence set back in as we slowly got closer.

When we finally pulled up next to them Poppy suddenly broke out in his usual loud happy high-pitched voice. 'Hello, how are you?' He smiled and greeted them as normal through the passenger-seat window. The cattle station owners gave us a curious hello and how are you going, but were looking at us very suspiciously. They already knew we wanted to light fires and the old fellas getting the land handed back was a totally new thing for them to swallow.

They asked us what we were doing and Poppy replied that we were camping and fishing. The cattle farmers then looked directly at me and said, 'You fellas haven't been lighting any fires, have you?' All three of us shook our heads and said at the same time, 'Nah.' The conversation didn't go far after that before Poppy said, 'Alright then, we gonna go now.' Old TG nudged me to jump out and throw our swags and bags in the back tray of the Toyota. We then started driving off, waving and saying goodbye as we made our escape.

We only drove about two hundred metres away when Poppy looked in the back tray and saw that his bag wasn't there. It was still sitting next to an ironwood tree at our camp, right next to where the cattle owners were standing. I started to turn the car around to retrieve it, but Poppy said, 'No, don't go back.' Instead, he asked me to run back to get the bag. Sitting in the middle seat, old man TG was in agreement, poking me in the ribs to get me going and to make it quick. I was totally freaked out by the idea, but took a deep breath, jumped out of the truck and started running.

I was about halfway when I saw the pastoralists looking curiously in the direction of our fire. When I looked through the trees I could see the gentle white smoke starting to ooze beautifully through the trees. I could see that the pastoralists were looking right at it, pointing at the thin white haze of smoke. I was instantly under attack. The old station owners looked at me and shouted, 'You! You've been lighting fires! I told you no fires!' I broke into a faster run, straight to Poppy's bag.

There were more swear words and angriness coming at me as I grabbed the bag. Once I had it in my hand I stopped and spoke to them in the nicest way I could. 'It's okay, just give them old men a chance. They know what they're doing.' That was all I said and then I ran back to the truck, still hearing their grumbling following behind me. There was no point in me saying anything else because they wouldn't listen to me anyway. When I got back to the car the old men were sitting in there moaning 'Oh no.' I threw the bag in the back and drove off, with the old men sitting in dead silence once again.

We all kept looking back to see if the cattle owners were following us, but we were pretty much out of there. That day was the longest drive home from country we had ever done. I found myself constantly asking the old fellas if everything would be okay. Poppy answered yes, and repeated again how the fire would be good and would not travel far. I took his word for it, but then those silent moments would come again, playing with my mind for the worst.

Eventually we got to a hilly point of the road and Poppy told me to stop the car. From the hill we could see all of their country stretching into the distance. He pointed in a direction and far away in one little pocket of the massive landscape was our little puff of white smoke, doing its thing. The view was beautiful and it was at that moment that I started to feel proud of what we had done. Old TG gazed over the distance and commented in support of his older brother, 'That's good. That old man knows what he's doing. You gotta burn the country.' Then Poppy once again assured me that the fire was fine, then he gave the final hand signal of the day to drive on home.

From that day on for the next month, things were pretty full-on. My home phone was starting to ring a few too many times, but I wouldn't answer it. It was either national parks or some cattle property owner ringing to chase me down. There were rumours coming from national parks staff that I was in big trouble. Bad messages from the pastoralists were passed on to me through the grapevine, and stories grew taller, saying that our fire was nothing but bad. It was sounding worse and worse as the days went by. All we did was one little fire that did exactly what the old man said it would do. It burnt one little ecosystem that was ready to burn, seen through the eyes of Indigenous knowledge.

They didn't seem to blame the Elders, they were blaming me as the troublemaker because I was the young outsider. It was my head they wanted and that was the easy way for them to deal with it. If they got rid of me then the whole fire thing with the Elders would simply go away. The tall stories about our burn started to make me angry, so I started to plan my response. I figured it was pointless to try and face them with words, but I had another idea.

First, a little backstory: in 1996 the local Aboriginal Corporation got a video camera and a computer as part of an initiative to document Aboriginal stories. The ranger job I was doing gave me the chance to get out on country with the camera all the time. It was just a basic set-up, a DV tape handycam with no tripod, no microphone and a cord to connect to the computer. I had some previous camera experience from the old VHS tape cameras I played with at school.

I came to think that not only could we record stories but also film cultural practices and traditional knowledge. It could only be a good idea, I could see that the younger ones weren't picking up the information. I didn't think writing it down would be accurate enough for such a complex knowledge system, the old people couldn't read or write anyway. By videoing the interviews, the Elders could also view the clip to see if they got everything right, or if they had missed anything.

I told the Elders to pretend the video camera was one of their grandchildren, and that they would be able to learn from the film later too. That made sense to them and in no time they were getting stuck into doing the work. It was the closest thing to the traditional transfer of knowledge, where you could see them, hear them, and see the actions of a practice or preparation. There was no misinterpretation, or anyone else's interpretation – it was all coming from the source itself.

We would record anything that we saw on our journeys, from plants and animals, to places to practices. We would record the medicine use, the food use, the bushcraft use, the lore, the management, and the interrelationships including language names. We never needed to plan before the shoot and the first take was always the best take. There was an endless list of things to record, as the knowledge and stories were everywhere we looked in the landscape. We got pretty good at what we were doing and the old people were glowing with confidence. I would simply point my eyes at something and they would start talking about it from top to bottom, inside and out. Poppy would always finish his recording by saying, 'That's all I can say.'

The filming started to trigger their minds, unlocking the knowledge stored away in their heads over their lifetimes. If they couldn't remember something on one day, they would sleep on it and then tell me everything the next morning.

One day an educated stranger came around and told me about storing information on digital databases. He loaded a database program onto our project's computer, to show what it was all about. He taught me how to build a basic layout for a knowledge record and how to add more fields onto that. I started to build my own database, developing a place for each bit of information. I learnt how to edit the videos and put them into the layout where they belonged. It was the beginning of developing a basic map of an entire knowledge system.

I decided to give the national parks staff and pastoralists a film presentation on the fire work the Elders were doing, and got the Awu-Laya database ready to show them. During this time there were more rumours spreading around about what our fire did that day. One positive rumour came through saying that the pastoralists liked our burn because they could easily muster their cattle. Then the bad rumours would take over again.

A month later I was ready to face the music and organised a meeting to bring everyone together to sort the situation. I chose the local Ang-Gnarra Aboriginal Corporation office in Laura as the place. I set up the projector in the meeting room a little earlier, before everybody arrived. I left the screen on with the fire section of the database in full view for all to study when they entered the room. I then left the building and went down the road to see if any others from the community wanted to come along. When it was time I drove past the office to see if they had all arrived. They were all there alright, slowly making their way into the meeting room. Poppy and Old TG were with them too, along with the chairman of the corporation. Once they were all inside I drove into the car park and went to the back of the office to prepare. I wanted them to sit in there a little while and look at the screen prepared for them earlier. I took a few deep breaths and made my entrance into the room to make my appearance.

When I entered I saw that they were all sitting down looking at all the fire pictures and text on the screen. When they saw me they all went silent – you could hear a pin drop in the tiny room. I was expecting some yelling straight away, but the content on the screen may have worked a little. Without another moment wasted I started to tell the story of Aboriginal fire and the concerns the Elders had for their country. Poppy and old man TG started to back me up once the presentation got into the flow. They spoke with big smiles on their face and obvious signs of pride in their videos and pictures on the projected screen. We talked about recording traditional knowledge and all the reasons why the Elders wanted to look after the land. The small crowd was fixed, listening without a word to say. When I played a section of video the old men would say, 'That's me, see what I'm doing.' Then you would hear that high-pitched laugh of approval from Poppy. The rest of the people in the room just sat there with blank looks on their faces.

By the end of our presentation the audience said nothing, I stood there waiting to hear their thoughts but not one word or question came from their lips. With sounds of shuffling chairs, they all stood up and walked out of the room with not one glance back at me. I watched the huddled group make their way to the door muffling a word or two. I didn't want them to leave because I wanted to discuss ways forward, but I was glad with the outcome all the same.

As the last person closed the door behind them I was left standing there in an empty room. I breathed out a breath of relief and plonked into a chair for a moment of thought. I could feel a big smile starting to stretch across my face and automatically jumped up clapping my hands, and did a little victory dance around the room. But I quickly stopped dancing once I noticed that they could still see me through the office window.

It was from that day that I realised the power of traditional knowledge in the modern world we live in. A knowledge system based on natural lore from thousands of years of experience was a match for any man-made reality. No matter how long a farmer lived on the country and no matter how many university degrees the national parks staff had, they were not even close to understanding the knowledge of them old people. This got me excited; it was the first time I led a meeting and batted for the old people and their country and won the day. As I watched them all drive away I knew it wasn't the end of the battle – there was still a long way to go.

Chapter 5
The start of the season

Boxwood country and gum-tree country

When we did get to light fires we would burn the country according to the old ways of each different place. Poppy taught me about the ecosystems that would burn from the beginning of the year right through to the end of the fire seasons. In the early months of the year, after the wet season, the country was all green and you couldn't apply fire then. Even the storm burn country (discussed in Chapter 7) was too green to burn by then – if it wasn't full with years of dead fuel, that is. People ate lots of fruit and plant foods at that time because they were plentiful. Kangaroos and other small animals were a little harder to catch because the grass would be too long. The animals were also scattered all over the place because there was plenty of water and greenery around the landscape.

The people would wait for fire season to start, the time when they could put in their first burns. The first ecosystem ready to burn on Awu-Laya country is the boxwood tree system. Poppy would point out signs of flowering trees that signalled the start of certain systems. He pointed out the bloodwood trees' first flower of the year, which told him when the boxwood country was ready to burn. He pointed out many more interrelationships and signs that signified when animals were breeding, plants were fruiting, and when the seasons would come and go. These relational indicators are a very important part of reading the land and knowing when things are ready to burn and when they are not. It also helps to understand and adjust to climate and seasonal shifts each season.

So when it was time for the first burn in Awu-Laya country, we would go to the boxwood tree country. Poppy would jump out of the truck and walk into the country, always looking around with sharp eyes. He would say, 'You have to take notice all the time, know all the trees, and know the country. So you don't get lost.' He then grabbed a handful of the long grass and ran it through one hand to feel the moisture, to see if it was ready to burn. If the grass felt cold, there was too much moisture. If it felt warm and dry, it was ready. Then he showed me how to visually read the curing of the grass and when it was ready to burn. The grass was about half green and half dry when it was ready. All the seeds on the grass had already fallen off and settled onto the ground.

If the grass didn't have all of those signs, he wouldn't even bother striking a match. The time boxwood country is ready can be between late March and early May, depending on how good the rain season was. When we burned boxwood country at the right time, no other system would burn because they were still too green. They act as firebreaks, and the same rule applies to all the fire ecosystems if you burn them at the right time. The later burns would then stop where the earlier burns were done, and so on.

It is also extremely important to look for the right ignition point and light up respectfully. 'Don't put too much fire in this one, just enough to let it burn.' The boxwood fire was slightly bigger than most other burns because it is a very grassy system. Fire travels well in this country so you don't need too many ignitions. But still very cool and low, so that the trees and the canopy are not scorched or burnt.

'You can't burn this country too late, because it's too hot to burn, because the dirt is dark,' Poppy would say. Poppy would say that the dark soil would absorb heat and stunt all the seeds. That encourages the grasses, herbs and small plants to become sparse and not as plentiful. Even if you burn boxwood country in late winter it is no good, because the grass is drier and more flammable. If the grass is completely dry, then it is too late to burn the country. In the old men's Thaypan country, it is usually around mid April when this fire is applied. There is still moisture in the country from the wet season and there is a full winter of dew following to help reshoot vegetation. Burning too late with too much heat won't get the best regrowth response for this country and the trees will get burnt. The country will end up pretty bare throughout the year, until there is rain. Everything that depends on that country would find hardship as a result of unfavourable burning, or not burning at all. There is a narrow window with the timing to produce the right fire, to apply the right heat for the soils.

In the old days the Elders would say, 'Right, it's time to burn all the boxwood country.' A small group would go for a walkabout around their country and burn all the systems that were ready. The rest of the mob from the main camp could see their smoke and know where they were travelling. Seeing the smoke in the distance was a sign that the traditional firemen were doing their job in a certain selection of country all over, roaming from place to place, getting it ready for hunting and gathering grounds for later on.

Once the burning of the boxwood forests was finished, it was then time to start burning gum-tree country. The gum country was also one of the early systems to burn and it's found throughout Australia. For some people's country, it is the first system to burn, it all depends on what type of country you have in your area. Burning the gum-tree systems in Awu-Laya country meant that the fire season was well and truly on the way. The boxwood and gum country are usually the bigger systems that burn, compared to some other ecosystems that know fire. Gum-tree country has slightly lighter-coloured soil than the boxwood, and they share similar open, grassy areas, so the fire behaviours are also similar because of this.

There are many types of different gum-tree communities, but most of them have similar timing and indicators for burning. You can find massive big red gums and other species in the rainforest either, but fire is not applied there very often, if at all. There are also gum trees that live in river areas, like ghost gums, that don't see fire too. They are too important for the water and are crucial to the riverbanks of Australia. There are also the Moreton Bay ash type gums that like to have their feet wet at times of the year. Sometimes this gum country burns a little later in the season, because of its water connection. They produce a beautiful, thick, native grass with lush seeds. But most of the other open gum forests share the same burning time: from late April to early June, depending on the season and location.

Once the box and gum systems are burnt they start reshooting fresh grass shoots within a couple of weeks. Sometimes new shoots can start popping up within a day or two if the moisture is there. The country is now clean and the old grass has been taken away. The land becomes green and lush again for the second time in the year. These systems will now become healthy, green firebreaks for the neighbouring country that will burn later on. It will continue to support all the animals and plants that depend on the boxwood and gum communities throughout the rest of the year.

Stringybark country and sand-ridge country

Once the boxwood and gum country is finished, other ecosystems are curing to match a good time for their fire. Some country like stringybark and sand-ridge country provide an abundance of smaller food and medicine plants, shared with a few species of native grasses. These types of countries are special because of the many plants provided for the people and animals.

Fire is applied differently if these rich winter burn systems are plentiful with diverse food plants. If they are rich with many food plants and appear lush, then the old people would not burn them, even when the grass has cured to the right time, because you don't want to burn the food plants if there are plenty in there. If you burn all the food plants away it will make it hard to find food – hard to recognise vines and small plants that lead to yams and tubers underground.

But if there aren't many food plants and it is full of old grass that's smothering the ground, then it should be burnt in the right winter timing. This will help to reset the country and get the fuel loads down. It's important not to leave it too close to summer to burn, otherwise the land will not get enough moisture from the cold nights to regrow vegetation effectively.

In some country like the sandy stringybark systems, you can burn the grass and not harm many food plants. The timing needs to be spot-on and not too late. You have to be on country all the time to burn like this. Burn country like you are gardening for food, and like you are living off the land to survive. Because the old people did not burn that particular piece of winter country, they had access to plenty of bush foods. It would last through winter and into summer until many plants start to die off. If the country does not burn at the end of the winter season then it can then be done in the storm burn time, to spark food again for the rain season.

Sometimes if there's plenty of moisture and rain through the winter, you can burn some country twice in one year. Storm burn and then winter burn. Use the bush foods and medicines in the wintertime from the storm burn and then burn at the right time in winter to reshoot sources of plant foods that can be relied on through summer. These burns are only small-scale burns implemented in a similar way to gardening and harvesting. You need good rain or dew to burn like this, otherwise you will end up with bare country after the winter. Burning for food and burning to protect food is a constant aim in applying fire in rich food and medicine systems. Most people today have never thought about fire on the land this way, and these complex layers. It is a sophisticated form of land management based on creating food, much like permaculture.

It was the rich food and medicine places, like the sand-ridge and stringybark country, that I liked going to the most with Poppy and TG. It provided a wide range of bush supermarket products that could just about assist any common medical discomfort you could have. We would inspect and prepare ten different plants within a tiny square metre of country in the really healthy areas. The ground here had a nice, sandy soil, easy to dig and a nice place to sit and forage away.

Old man TG had lots of knowledge about plants in the sand-ridge country. He was like a bush doctor when it came to talking about the plants and their uses. He'd spot something and then casually stroll over and sit down cross-legged next to it. He would even talk to the plant in gratitude, just like talking to another countryman, with his long, old-aged fingers slowly digging into the sandy soil to pull out roots or tubers. We would make the medicines whenever we could and try them all out as a way to practice.

The flames in the stringybark country should transpose these two words along the trails of dry, dead grass weaving through the system, burning pathways and leaving smaller patches of greener plants unburnt. The right fire in this system should trickle like water, moving slowly, servicing the country. The flames are no more than a few inches high as they gradually turn the dead vegetation into thin, black ash. Such a beautiful thing, watching a proper stringybark fire take place.

A healthy stringybark fire makes thin, white smoke rather than flames when lit the right way. This time is the late winter season – for most places one of the last systems to burn for the winter season. Burning this country at a cold, dewy time of year makes sense, because the stringybark tree is too flammable in drier times. When fire goes around the stringybark tree, it will sometimes burn a little way up the tree, but it doesn't hurt it. The fire will only burn the old bits of bark on the surface and then extinguish itself. It is one of my favourite fires, getting to see those tall stringybark trees in the misty grass smoke. They look like tall spirits standing there, with their shimmering leaves bathing in light white smoke.

When fire is applied in stringybark country properly, you can't tell that it has been burnt when you look from far away. You only notice when you get close and start walking inside, under the canopy. It doesn't take long before more ground plants grow after the fire and replace the old, dead fuel.

There are different types of stringybark country as well. There is stringybark country that has very low canopies and lives on stony, hard, hilly country. This type of stony stringybark is burnt in the storm season, or when plenty of rain comes. Another one lives in the reddish basalt soils, which also burns in the winter season. They also live in mixed-tree systems, which are usually the last systems we burn in Awu-Laya country. But the best stringybark country for me is still on the sandy soils, the taller, mystical stringybark trees.

Sand-ridge, river country, stringybark and bloodwood trees that live in the sandy soils are all places of harvesting food and medicine plants. When I am in this type of country I can see images in my mind of women and children foraging around. It is always shady and cool in these places too. Poppy told me that women can burn these richer systems, because they were associated with it through the gathering of resources.

It is good to bring the whole family when visiting this country, because there is a connection to resources for everyone. I love walking people through this country and giving them a tour of all the different plants. There is so much knowledge and stories to share. There are other country types on the coastal areas and inland that also burn in wintertime. Getting them healthy will make it easier to demonstrate the different burns for each particular system, keeping the winter burn countries greener and with low fuel loads through the summer season.

Chapter 6
Mixed-tree country

One random category of country that takes time to understand is the mixed-tree country. You need a good understanding of the trees and their relationship values to understand the story. The name mixed-tree country was taught to me by Poppy, who explained to me how the country is broken up into more ecosystems than what we see. A bit like how there are more seasons in Indigenous weather calendars compared with the Western version, which only has four.

There are many types of mixed-tree country that exist in the fire-dependent ecosystems. This country has different types of trees growing in it, which makes each mixed-tree system different to the next mixed-tree system, depending on the mix of parent trees and what country they represent. Full-blood country is when a system has only one type of parent tree that makes up the country. Like a full gum-tree forest or a full stringybark tree forest. Then as soon as one different tree comes into the mix, the country starts to change. The soils start to change, and the species of vegetation, and the curing of the grass has a different timing. The values for the system change and it is then considered a different country. Mixed-tree country is like a transition country between all the many types of full-blood systems.

Again, you have to be on country all the time to put fire like this into it. 'This mix tree country is more hard to burn, because it is a story country', Poppy would say. It was a special place because it would burn and cure later, and sometimes wouldn't burn at all. Poppy showed me

40

a place that had all gum trees living in it. Then he showed me where the bloodwood trees started to come into the mix and transform the country. The grass in the gum-tree country was drier than the vegetation in the gum and bloodwood forest. If you burnt the full gum-tree forest at the right time, then the fire would stop and go out when it got to the mixed gum and bloodwood country.

Some mixed-tree country would be ready to burn in the early winter season, and some mixed-tree country would be ready to burn in the late winter season. It all depends on what trees are in the mixed-tree country, which indicates which one should burn before the other. If the mixture of trees change again into mixed gum and boxwood, that system would burn earlier than the mixed gum and bloodwood system. The boxwood tree is from the country that has the first burns of the year.

The different trees in mixed-tree country also change the qualities in the soils, too. The different trees will bring their soil characteristics to combine as one, to make up the country for the particular place. The gum tree will have a dark, grey soil, while the bloodwood tree coming in would bring a lighter, sandier soil quality. The soils then mix together to create the soil type for that system. If you add a stringybark to the list then you get an even sandy type of soil. If you then take out the gum tree the soil becomes even looser and lighter in colour. If you add an iron bark tree then there will be stones and rocks mixing in.

There are so many different systems when you read the country this way. Understanding mixed-tree country is important to ensure the fire doesn't get away – so you know what country will not burn. You will also know where it is safe to be while watching the fire do its natural thing. If you don't know the land, the trees, and the order they cure in then you won't understand mixed-tree country properly. Usually it is certain stringybark, tea-tree or bloodwood mixed-tree country in the moist, sandy soils that is best to burn last in the winter season.

By spring many of the winter systems have been burnt and have grown green again, ready for some animals to breed and feed on the diverse vegetation. Many plants bloom and animals breed in the springtime, and many bloom and breed at other times of the year too. This is why the mosaic pattern of burning country is important to support the diversity and needs of different species.

It is perfectly locked together in connectedness. When spring did arrive much of the lowland, richer soil systems were burnt in the old days. All of the burnt winter country would then have far less chance of a wildfire coming through in summer. The river systems, rainforest and other no-fire systems would also be locked off and surrounded by the winter burn country, keeping them safe from the wildfire in summer as well. The only place that should have dry, dead grass in summertime is the storm burn country in poorer-quality, rockier soils. There would also be some winter country that has been missed too, but that is okay because most of the country would have been treated.

When spring comes along, the climate starts to heat up a bit. By October it was known to be too hot to burn in most places in Awu-Laya country. But, of course, the burning windows are different now and shift a little depending on place and climate. Burning time is over when the heat kicks in, and if you haven't burnt the early season country in time, then it must wait until you can do careful storm burning, or until the next winter season. You generally can't burn country if you have passed its proper burning time. Otherwise you will do more damage than good to the country. This means that the country misses out on its burn, but it is not a bad thing if it is healthy country.

But if it is neglected country, with a build-up of lots of fuel, then there are problems in many different ways. The worst thing that can happen is a wildfire setting off an accumulating, ticking time bomb. If that doesn't happen, in the long run it means a lack of food and medicine plants due to oppressive, dry fuel loads.

This is why it is important to burn at the right time, knowing that you have to be on country all the time to read the indicators. The burning window for all the winter fire season in Thaypan country can go from April to August, which can mean up to four to five months of looking after the country. When you burn this way, the fires are smaller, lower in intensity, and there are many more of them. If you manage all your country properly, then there should be an abundance of food and healthy country.

The important part to understand is that it is harder to manage the country like this if it has years of fuel and weeds dominating. Different burning styles and work will be needed when the land is sick like this. Getting the country healthy will make the diverse curing of the landscape more visible, making it easier to know when to burn and contain the fire next time. In the long run, fire management should become easier and the burns a lot safer if the curing knowledge on timing is correctly followed.

Chapter 7
Storm burn country

Once springtime is over, it is then time for the dry, hot season to slowly arrive. That's the time for the build-up season, waiting for the big rain to come. But it will be a long, hot, dry season before that happens. It wasn't so bad because the hot time was good for plenty of fishing and pig hunting, as the rivers became warmer and the water levels got lower. We would be more focused on hunting at this time of year, and most of the family would come out, knowing that there was a sure catch of bush tucker. The four-wheel drives were always packed with the families in the back tray, buckets of fishing lines and dogs bouncing around as we hit the dusty roads to favourite waterholes. Everyone came out onto country in those days, because it was still legal to travel in the back tray of a four-wheel drive.

Just because it was dry season, it didn't mean that we stopped talking about fire. The old fellas continued to talk about storm burning – burning in the late, dry times of the year before the main wet season. One particular country that is good for storm burning is ironbark country. Ironbark trees usually bring stony country, with a reddish, blueish, metal tinge. The rocks conduct heat like hot plates and the larger stones are good for ground oven cooking. Sometimes the rocks can have a hard, sandstone-like quality to them too. One day we drove past that country and asked Poppy if it needed to be burnt. He responded with a quick 'Nah … You can't burn that country like the other ones. You can only burn it when there's a lot of rain.'

He signalled me to stop the car and we walked out to the middle of the hard, stony, clayish ground. The old man started explaining that you have to wait for the first or second rain before you can burn that country. You need to make sure there is plenty of moisture in the soil. 'If you burn it when it is dry, nothing will grow again for a long time.' He started digging into the hard soil with a sharp stick that he picked up from the ground. 'See how it is dry? That's no good.' He went on to say that you have to have moisture in the soil to at least a half a foot to a foot deep. Then you can burn it and the vegetation will come back quicker and thicker.

We then travelled on to another type of storm burn country which was more in the hilly areas. The soil in this country is also very hard, and whitish in colour. It also had lots of the same reddish stones, including lots of white quartz and ochre. I also noticed that there were boxwood, gum, bloodwood and stringybark trees on this country. They were a lot smaller than the usual trees of their type in the darker, richer soils. I asked the old man why they weren't in their proper place. Poppy responded that it was devil devil country. 'This place is trying to trick you by putting different trees that burn early on top.' If you burn this place like the winter country, nothing will grow again all year. It will stay bald and dry.

The small, yellow-leafed quinine tree is another system that needs the rain when it is dominating in its place. You can commonly find this type of quinine tree in sand-ridge country too with the winter trees. But when he is dominating he usually has a hard, stony ground which puts the system in the storm burn category. Being that these country types have hard, stony ground, it makes sense why the country needs a foot of rain in the soil before applying the burn.

Storm burn country can be found in lowlands, but also commonly in escarpments and ridge lines. It is always known as hard country. It was not usually a place where all the tribe would hang out most of the year. The land is usually uneven and there are lots of rocks and holes to break your ankle and injure yourself. There is hardly any water in this country and in the hot time you can barely walk on the scalding ground that attracts heat from the burning sun. Not a good place for the old people and children to camp on.

The country does have its uses, though, just like everything that is produced by nature. Some of the country provides good, high ground from the flood seasons. There are also good caves and rock shelters that were commonly used during the wet-season times. Rock art is still commonly found in the high country rock escarpments, marking these camps today. The ridge lines were also walking trails to allow easy travel from one place to another. The storm burn country is ready to burn right at the time when the walking trails will be used for high ground. Walking and burning from these trails is very important for many communities that have this type of country. To look after the cultural heritage and to be able to access the old walking trails again that connected one place to the other.

The storm burn country can supply great stone quarries for making tools, knapping stones and flint into knives and spear tips. The stringybark and boxwood trees growing in this country are usually hollow, making them a good place to find a didgeridoo. You can also find medicine and food there, but it is not an ideal place for hunting and gathering. It has fruit trees in the wet season, which also matches up perfectly with people being there at that time, in shelter. But like all other country, it is highly respected and valued for what it is and is managed just the same.

The problem we have with this country in modern times is that we are often prevented from demonstrating how to burn it, because all the government agencies and landholders would freak out with a fire being lit at the end of the drier times of the year. There have been times when the first rains have come up north and storm burn country is ready to burn safely. But wildfires are still burning down south, which makes the wardens up north nervous as well. They don't realise that you need to wait for the rain, and the right amount as well. When the gullies and creeks, and even some swamp areas, go completely green again, it indicates there's moisture is in the harder soils. The lower, richer system then becomes a fire break for the storm burn country. If the burn is left too late into the wet season, the land can get too green to burn and can miss its timing. I am always determined to manage and demonstrate the burns on storm burn country because it is another burning window that people are less aware of.

After the right amount of rain and all the indicators are showing that it is ready to burn, it is like a change in the summer season. The country is now ready for fire again. The native grasses begin to burn calmly even though there is still lots of dry grass in the storm burn systems. The dry grass sucks up the moisture from the damp soils even when its dead, making the fire cooler. Most dead vegetation will suck up moisture at different times of the year and that is an advantage for burning techniques. You need to be careful on your ignition points in a storm burn because lighting it the wrong way can make the fire flare up. It is still warmer weather than in the winter months, but the fire can't go far with green winter country and creeks around.

In northern Australia the storm burns are usually at the end of the year, but you can apply fire to storm burn country any time of the year, as long as you have plenty of rain. Depending on your location, if you get lots of rain you should take advantage no matter what time of the year. This is the same for most systems that can also be shifted depending on changes in weather and climate. The indicators in the country matching with shifting seasons will show you how to adjust your fire for the right place. I love burning in storm burn time, when big rain clouds are brewing up for the afternoon to come and meet the fire. It is a magical to experience.

Over many trips on country the old men were getting sharper on their memories of knowledge and fire. We also connected with Elders from other communities who lived on the coast and further north of the region. They showed us how to burn areas you couldn't find on Awu-Laya country, like rainforest, coastal systems and bauxite country. We also shared the traditional knowledge work we were doing and how we were using a video camera. I got to know many great Elders from all over Far North Queensland, so beautiful and true; many have now passed. They all loved and supported the work we were doing, with Poppy and TG leading the way.

Chapter 8
No-fire country

When it comes to Aboriginal fire management, the old people didn't burn every ecosystem. Many people think that Aboriginal people burnt everything and applied fires that scorched large tracts of land. They also think it is like Western hazard reduction, but it is all far from the truth. How could they maintain the diversity of ecosystems and natural resources for thousands of years through the careless application of fire? Aboriginal fire knowledge is based on country that needs fire, and also country that doesn't need fire. Even country we don't burn is an important part of fire management knowledge and must be within the expertise of a fire practitioner.

You can find country that doesn't need fire in just about every region of Australia. Country we don't burn can be found in dry country, wet country, up in the mountains, and down in the valleys. There are so many places that don't need fire and we protect them by burning the places that need fire. To look after any ecosystem, you need to manage all the different country around it. If you don't manage the places that need fire, then the no-fire systems come under threat.

One of the obvious landscapes where people think fire is not so popular is the rainforest country. Much of the wet rainforest is no place for fire and it doesn't need burning to stay healthy. But there are types of rainforest country where Aboriginal people did apply fire. These types are more the dry rainforest, rather than the thick, wet forests. They tend to have more of a sandy soil and are mainly found in the lower river and coastal areas of the country. The fires I have experienced in these areas are among the slowest fires. They take off the cool, moist fuel loads to allow fresh vegetation to grow.

A dear old lady I know from the rainforest told me how her Elders burnt this type of dry sandy-soiled rainforest country. The last time she saw this type of fire happen was when she was a little girl. She took me for a walk, pointing out the way we were crunching on a blanket of dry leaves that she believed should be a mixed, sandy soil. As a little girl, she remembered when there was grass and other small plants that used to grow there. Her Elders burnt the area regularly to maintain the green vegetation for rainforest wallabies and tree kangaroos. There used to be plenty of those animals, but today she rarely sees any, since their Elders stopped managing the land.

We searched the area for evidence of a kangaroo family, but there was hardly a sign. The old lady made it clear that the animals were gone because there was no food for them. Not only was there a lack of food on the ground, but also in the trees. That day we started a small burn and then went on to treat other areas with the local rangers. When this country burns, the fire moves slowly and the flame is less than a foot above the litter. It is important that the fire does not harm the trees, so it is done when the leaves have some moisture, in the cooler seasons. There are only small pockets of this type of country and the burns I've seen have only been in small, concentrated areas.

Another special no-fire place the old people showed me is the spurs or gullies that run down the sides of mountains and escarpments. They are usually formed by water and most of them have permanent or seasonal springs. One day I walked into one of these gullies in sandstone escarpment country with the old men. The country around the hillside was dry stringybark and bloodwood forests that needed fire. When we walked down into the gully from the top of the hillside, the country changed dramatically. Instantly the temperature dropped by ten degrees and it was welcomed natural air conditioning at any time of the year.

The thick leaf litter belongs on this ground and should never get to see any fire, or as little as possible. Most of the no-fire systems we don't burn naturally have a leafy forest floor and are the only places where this type of understory is welcomed. There are animals that depend on the leaf litter and its moisture at most times of the year. The old man pointed out a big scrub turkey nest, which is a large mound of leaves raked up by the busy bird. 'Look there, boy – it's a fresh one too. Check the nest for any eggs.' Old TG stuck his hand into the giant mound of leaves to feel if it was warm inside. If it is warm inside then it is a sign that there are eggs. 'Yeah, boy, they're there alright.' We started to dig to find the eggs one at a time, just enough for ourselves to take home for dinner.

The mother turkey lays her eggs in separate places so that goannas and other predators don't find them all in one spot. There was no way we were going to dig the whole nest to find them all – it was way too big. Plus you need to be careful of digging up a snake, because they like nesting in them warm scrub turkey mounds too. Once we had finished collecting a couple of eggs the old man then showed me some plants that he had never taught me about before. They could only be found in these special areas that provide the right cool, dark conditions for them to grow. They were very special medicines which treated certain health conditions that were quite unusual to the common health conditions. There are also parent trees that don't need fire, like the paperbark trees, Leichhardt tree, and umbrella trees, to name a few. Besides those types of trees there are also gums, bloodwoods and stringybarks that happily blend into this type of country.

When you burn the surrounding fire-dependent systems at the right time the leaf litter in the no-fire systems will hold too much moisture for it to burn. The fire burning in the surrounding country will go out at the edge of the leaves every time. The only condition for this to be guaranteed is that the surrounding country that needs fire burns at precisely the right time. It is another example of how everything in Mother Nature is in sync, falling into place with the right timing of applying fire. It is amazing how Mother Nature provides the exact right conditions for each country to bring the right fire and also stop the right fire. Different vegetation types are more flammable than others at different times of the year for an important reason: to provide the exact right fire management that doesn't burn everything at once and doesn't burn no-fire country. All no-fire country has built a resistance to fire and will extinguish it only if the fire in the surrounding country is applied at the right time. Otherwise the fire-sensitive systems in the no-fire country cannot hold back the fire and will burn if they are under extreme conditions and are unmanaged.

There are a number of naturally leafy ecosystems found in the drier areas of northern Australia that have the same lores on the prevention of any fire at all. The trees are usually a range of very thin-trunked species with very low canopies. There are also a few poisonous trees that live in this country too, that you don't want to mess with. The leaves are round and small and are very light, and easy to kick your feet through. This country is mainly found along rivers and floodplains, and I have walked through it on many fishing occasions with Poppy. You have to watch out for death adders, though. Leafy no-fire country is a good home for them. Our eyes are always peeled when we carry big barramundi back to our camp through these places.

Another system on the no-burn list is the full-blood she-oak trees that are found on coastal and inland areas. The she-oak or casuarina is a special tree and is sort of like a pine tree. It has leaves like pine needles that cover the ground floor leaving nothing else to grow within its domain. Once again, the fire will go out at the edges if the surrounding country is burnt at the right time. This tree has a special relationship with the wind and makes high-pitched whistling tones when it passes through the broom-like leaves. Because these systems are connected with the wind, they are refreshingly cool to sit under. Because of this they were often used as camps at certain times of the year outside of the wet season.

They made good camp areas because the ground can be cleared easily to a nice, white, sandy floor by simply scooping up the dead pine needles. You don't have to pull out grass to make a nice, clean ground floor, which is easier than most other places good for camping. Because the sandy floor is white, it lights up the ground at night, making it easy to see snakes coming through in the dark. Keeping the ground clean around the camp areas is often preferred, rather than having dry grass and debris there.

When you find these full-blood systems along the coastline it is common to find shell middens nearby. Shell middens are cultural sites where, over thousands of years, the people discarded varieties of shellfish shells after they had been eaten. The midden sites are a sign of how these popular camping areas represent feasting. The middens are like rubbish bins where the shells were not thrown anywhere, but kept in one place. You can't just throw bones and shells anywhere around the country, everything needs to go into its intended place by lore. Plus you don't want scavenging insects and animals coming into the camp. So when people throw any rubbish on the ground today, you are breaking Aboriginal lore. That's why it is important for young people to know this – even keeping your country clean from rubbish is exercising cultural practice. The young people need to know this so they can start putting the lore back, to strengthen cultural identity. That's why the she-oak tree is so special, because it brings these types of stories and knowledge. Because the old people camped under them, their spirit is still there today, sitting in the shade. Burning the trees brings bad luck, so not burning this country goes hand in hand with looking after it both environmentally and spiritually.

The she-oak also belongs in other mixed-tree countries and the sand-ridge system. They provide better quality seeds for animals like the black cockatoo. When the she-oak live in these systems in balance with other trees, they then belong to the sand-ridge fire. Burning at the right time will ensure that the she-oak are never harmed by the fire. The needles on the ground will still protect them from the fire, and allow it to pass without damage. Sometimes it will gently burn the needles, but that doesn't harm them at all. In the wrong country the she-oak can be an invasive native, so it is important to know where the fire fits in with this tree and when it doesn't.

There is a place where you can find she-oak trees in a mixed-system country that is a no-fire place. This type of country is found along the river systems.

The riverbanks and plains are also a common no-fire environment. They provide natural firebreaks because they are always green when all winter systems are ready to burn. The river holds many special plants and has a number of trees that have food and medicine sources. You can find lots of fruits in the wet season time, and many animals can be found there and hunted in the drier seasons. Even rivers and springs that are seasonal are still valued the same way. The river areas are protected from fire because the water is so important for all life. Like all of the five elements (fire, water, earth, wind and the cosmos), they are all equally important as each other.

It is crucial that fire is kept out of the rivers and springs to protect the parent water trees. The water trees that live on the banks of rivers, swamps and springs are so important to the health of our precious waterways. The big old paperbark, red paperbark, ghost gums, red gums and coolabahs are just a few of those important trees. They are all extremely valuable to the lifeblood of our Mother Earth, which is the water. Water, water, everywhere, cool and fresh. The blood of our mother, running through her veins and flowing into the massive waterway chambers of her heart. Without the water trees, our water will start to find it hard to stay on country to play its role of supporting life.

One night Poppy told me a story that massive water trees were once all over the landscape. But now many of them have been destroyed by wildfires that rage through unmanaged country. If the people of today had looked after the country that needs fire, then the water trees would still be here today. Their unfortunate absence leaves behind dry waterholes with no shade, exposed to the sun to dry up what is left. Dead trunks of what used to be beautiful trees are left standing on the riverbanks, giving no more shade. Some of them have fallen into the dirty waters, left there to rot as the banks erode away. What used to be a cool, nurturing place that supported life is now neglected and ruined – left to the fate of bad land, water and fire management.

Late-season fires run straight through rivers when unmanaged land is full of old, dry fuel. The big, old paperbark trees just need one spark to engulf them in flames, burning their bright, white trunks into looking like black-wilted matchsticks. No one seems to realise what has been lost when it comes to the death of our water trees. Restoring the health of the river ways will take generations, but it is a vital task that must happen. Water is a living thing, it is not a dead substance. In fact, if it was dead it would be polluted, green like pea soup, and make you sick when you drink it. If you can drink it and it is clean and fresh, it is alive and good for you and for everything else we share the planet with.

I was told by a respected Elder that if you mistreat water, it will run away. It will dry up, go underground, leaving an empty waterhole behind with maybe some stagnant water left for desperation. Fire and water go together; preserving our water goes hand in hand with looking after the land with fire. When the fire country is mistreated from wildfires and bad burning, there is no vegetation left but bare dirt. Then when it does rain, the water washes the topsoil into our rivers, which slowly muddies up the riverbeds and shallows the waters. The fire country from high and low terrains needs healthy vegetation to hold the soils together, to stop them eroding into the rivers.

Even though much of the river country is protected from fire, there are also times when the fire burns right to the riverbank's edge. Poppy and old TG would burn country as we went fishing from time to time. Nothing feels better than fishing while the country is slowly burning near the riverbank. But the only time the fire burns right to the riverbank is when the parent trees from the fire country grow right up to the bank. Then the bank of the river will usually be a steep drop-off to the water; just like the land has suddenly broken off, leaving the river right there below the steep bank. The grasses from the fire country will also grow right to the edge, following the fire trees.

If you see that the riverbank has a gradual, steady, flat slope, then it is good not to apply fire in those areas. Instead, those types of riverbanks hold many different types of special trees and water-based vegetation. Low riverbanks like this should have dark, rich soils or river sand that gradually lead up to the other country types. Because of the soils and the gradual, shallow banks, the water is able to seep through a little way, forming the river country we don't burn. Water grasses, trees and other small shrub plants grow in these areas, forming a range of different riparian systems. This typical riverbank will usually stay green for most of the year and form a natural firebreak to protect itself. It's a buffer between the land and the river, creating a moist vegetation playground for water-dependent animals like frogs, to name one out of many. Having healthy river systems with flowing water makes it easier to manage the rest of the country with fire.

The banks of the wetlands and lagoons have the same kind of gradual slopes that gently connect to the dry land country. When the dry season comes, the water recedes, leaving behind dry, dead water grasses and reeds. Fire is applied to these types of waterways when they dry up before the wet season. I have seen old ladies burn the dry edges of lagoon country to hunt for freshwater turtles that hibernate under the mud for a cool, sleepy summer. Burning away not only clears the ground so you can see through the dry cracks in the mud, but also prepares the ground for the plants to reshoot next season. Doing this type of burn in the late season is once again done safely when all the surrounding fire country is managed properly.

One of the no-fire countries I like visiting a lot is the saltwater, muddy mangrove country. I love the mangrove country up north because of the bush tucker that comes out of this special place. Mud crabs, fish, shells, mussels, snails and mangrove worms. Like many people, I rave about this place for its amazing seafood. But although the mangroves don't need the fire, there are surrounding small patches of country that don't mind the right burn. These are the surrounding saltwater grassy areas that create little grass plains within the mangrove estuary systems. Fire at the right time will always end up with a good result of healthy regrowth in these areas. I love burning them while I am fishing because the smoke chases away the mosquitoes.

But if you go to the coastal areas with beautiful sand dunes and beaches instead of mangroves, you will also find country that can be sensitive to fire. There are amazing fringes of beach plants that grow on the high tide lines of the coastal areas. They like to form a thin wall between the beach and the inland country. These areas are sensitive to fire and if the trees do get burnt then it takes a long time for them to recover. Fire will kill them very easily and this is why it is not good to burn them. They are useful to keep the sand together and prevent erosion, and create a good windbreak to camp behind. There are also different beach vines that grow along the sandy beaches that give food and medicine in these coastal areas.

But there are times when grass grows right up next to the beach and in some places it is good to carefully burn them. You can also find the shell middens nearby in these cases. It is good to make sure the fire is as light as possible to simply clear out the dry grass. It is also good to clear around shell midden sites before the burn if they have lots of dry fuel covering them. A hot fire can make those old white shells brittle and degrade them even faster. It takes time to care for cultural heritage sites when burning, but it has to be done.

Another diverse system that lives on the coastal shores is the heath country. This system is a special one, because it is one of a few systems that has different country in one country. First you have the wetlands that sometimes can be in these places. Nice, green swamp grasses surround little waterholes, which can also have a kind of peat or lichen growing on the ground. These plants are very sensitive to fire and it is really important that they don't burn. To protect them, you have to apply the right fire management for the other ecosystems that share heath country. One of them is the sandy country that has grasses and trees like banksias, pandanus, paperbarks, native fruit trees, and other saltwater shrubs. There is plenty of food and medicine in the sandy heath-like systems on the coast and applying fire in this country is done selectively and delicately.

Most people that talk about the heath community are too scared to burn it because of its flammability. As a result, these places rarely get burned and that is bad because it then builds up more fuel loads to create a time bomb at any time of the year. Then the fire-sensitive areas within the country become even more at risk of being destroyed. The leaf litter and dead plants that build up over the years become very thick and layered to support very little diversity. When it gets to this point, the banksias start to struggle and die off from a lack of fire, adding to the dangerous fuel loads.

Some people think that the banksia needs a hot fire so it is good to burn the heath really hot, with all the vegetation going up in smoke. It's not a good idea to manage country just for one species while the other plants and animals suffer from the same fire. Burning the sandy banksia country is done with a cool fire that cleans up the understory of this low-canopy system. This is usually at a time in winter when the wetland systems have plenty of water and moist surrounding soil to protect the peat and green swamp grass areas. The banksia loves the fire and will create its own heat for itself rather than all the vegetation suffering from a big hot fire right through.

When the cool fire goes under the banksia, the dead leaves around it start to pick up the flame height a little. The banksia will then suck up the fire and engulf itself in flames, creating heat to germinate its hard seeds. Everywhere else in the sandy system has a cool fire and then there are these sudden flare-ups from the banksia sucking up the fire to bathe in the hot flames. I sit and watch this happen often and it's incredible. It's like the banksia lets out some kind of invisible, flammable chemical that excites the fire to flare up into its branches. There so many different types of banksias, but most I have known live in fire country.

Another country that lives with the heath country is a stony, sandy bloodwood country. It can sometimes create little hills, and it burns later than the sandy heath country. Most times it will be too green to burn in the early winter times of the sandy banksia country, and takes its turn later than the sandy banksia system. This country, will generally be around the edges of the heath country and keeps the right fire in the sandy banksia area contained within itself.

Burning this country over all takes regular visits, because you are applying two or three fires at different times, making sure that you protect the no-fire saltwater swamps and the sensitive plants that don't like the fire to go out of control. To burn this place you have to walk through the whole system, as the swampy country and white sandy trails will break up the fire-dependent areas. More time and respect for this country is needed to manage it properly. As a plentiful country of resources, the people would walk through it regularly, which made it efficient to burn little places here and there throughout the seasons.

Overall, no-fire ecosystems are special places; it is important that we are protecting them and ensuring they are healthy and safe. There is a lot to learn about these places and why they are so significant, both environmentally and culturally. It is amazing how Mother Nature has created the balance of no-fire and fire-dependent systems to provide tolerance and courtesy between them through fire. It is all based on learning how it all comes together, to apply fire or not apply fire in a way that respects all the plants and animals that live in these places.

Chapter 9
Through the trees

When I went to visit country in the southern areas of Australia, the first thing I noticed was that the land was the same, but different. I could see the similarities in the country from the north to the south. For example, you can find a stringybark tree in northern Australia and you can find a stringybark tree in southern Australia. They may be different species of stringybark tree, but they are still stringybark trees. I noticed the same thing with many other tree species and ecosystems too. I saw similar grasses, plants, animals and soils. There were still some different plants and weeds compared to what we had in the north, but I could still read the country the same way.

Everywhere I went I dug into the soils and inspected the trees, finding comparisons within the landscape. I was starting to see what Poppy had told me about being able to read country in a different place. How the country shows you what to do when you read it and take notice of the signs. Everywhere I looked there were knowledge indicators within the landscape poking out everywhere, through the guidance of the trees.

The trees are the key to reading country, they are like the traditional Elders of each individual ecosystem. They tell what the place should look like and what animals and plants should be living there. To know this is understanding the bush food, medicine and bushcraft knowledge that is attached to each place. The old people occasionally asked me to go and get a certain plant or animal from the country for them. The first thing to do is to instantly go to the right place by reading the trees to find the country that has the resource.

There is a large diversity of ecosystems in the landscape – each have their own special characteristics and treasures. Learning all the trees and medicines is a must for understanding how to apply the right fire for the right country. The old people managed the country that needed fire in a certain way, to keep the diversity of ecosystems. As a result, the people and the animals had access to all the places that could supply particular resources they needed to survive.

The parent trees are like clan groups. They all have their own communities, country, and their own lore. Sort of like gum-tree clan, bloodwood clan, boxwood clan, tea-tree clan, and a whole range of mixed-tree clans to name only a few. And the fire will behave differently in each ecosystem when it is applied at the right time of the year. The native grasses have evolved over thousands of years to customise the right fire for the country. They produce the right heat, the right speed and the unique nature of the fire needed for the soils to reproduce the right vegetation. On the sandy country the grass is very flammable and light, which makes the fire travel fast over the sand. Heavy grass or large volumes of fuel would burn too slowly and heat up the sand too much. Most of the vegetation has developed in a perfect way to encourage the right fire for the soil and country it lives on. If you don't have the right vegetation in the country then you will get the wrong fire, which will give the wrong results.

The tree communities that need fire have a special relationship with the grass. When the grass cures to the right condition, the old people will burn it to create new shoots. The grass will cure at different times for each country type, giving the signal for when each tree community is ready to burn. One by one each system burns and the other system with greener grass puts out the fire. Then, when the next system is ready to burn, the previous burnt country puts it out with its new green shoots. One by one throughout the season, each particular fire-related community gets its cleansing to remain rich, healthy and plentiful.

Most of the time, the grass is visually ready to burn when it is half green and half dry. Poppy showed me a second test where you run the grass through your hand to feel if it is ready. If the feeling of warm and dry runs through your hand then it is ready to burn. If it is cold and moist, then basically it is too early to burn. The trees tell us roughly what time we burn and then the grass indicates the exact right time. If there is no grass where there is supposed to be grass, then you need to rely on the soil and the trees.

There are different qualities of smoke that are used for medicine, communication, cooking, and spiritual uses. The old people made a strong point that when we burn country, the only thing that we intend to burn is the grass. The grass smoke helps with the flowering of the trees, to produce more seeds for germination. The trees bathe in the white smoke to improve their canopies, and the leaves give a gentle shimmering dance when the smoke comes into contact with them. The good, thin white, medicine smoke for the trees only comes from burning the grass.

When you stand in the grass smoke it doesn't make you cough or sting your eyes as much as other types of smoke. You will soon cough and show signs of discomfort if you become smothered in darker or black smoke produced from oil-based vegetation types other than grass. There are some grasses like spinifex that produce a stronger smoke, but the majority of native grasses produce the thin, white smoke. Burning the leaves of the canopy or old, dead leaf litter also produces a harsher, darker smoke. The black smoke will form a plume high in the sky and can stick around for a few days after the burn. The oil content from the trees is released into the atmosphere and that is not a good thing for the country. The chemical and oil contents within the trees are for cultural and medicinal uses, and not to be burned into the atmosphere.

On regular hunting trips with the old people, we would walk a long way through the landscape. Sometimes a major storm would start to brew to interrupt our hunting venture. It wasn't good because the rain was usually so heavy that it could flood rivers within minutes. We would then try and get home quickly, to avoid being flooded in. On many occasions the Elders would retaliate by collecting certain leaves from medicine plants that could produce smoke to clear the rain. 'Oh, look at that rain coming. Quick, lets burn some medicine to chase him away', they would say. They would tell us to collect the special leaves from a plant and then some bark off a certain tree to make the base of a fire. We would light the bark up and throw the fresh green leaves on top to send the dark, thick smoke up into the sky.

On many occasions I witnessed this practice, watching the smoke rise slowly into the sky. The black rain clouds heading towards us would simply split into two and go around us, leaving us nice and dry. I thought it was magic at first, but after a few times I came to realise that the chemicals coming from the smoke of the medicine plants was the key ingredient for the cultural practice. I have heard other people tell stories of rainmakers and stoppers through magical ceremony, and sometimes they were simply done through the power of the natural resources on their own.

It is not only bad for the country having the trees all burnt, but also bad for the atmosphere to take in all of those chemicals. There are so many connections of communication within the landscape – we have no idea of what they are capable of. The roots of the trees and plants create a whole connected web that communicate and support each other. The animals constantly talk with each other and leave signs in the landscape that forms a language within their shared kingdom. There are many frequencies of sound we don't hear or know of and they are all around us.

When the trees flower, they make sweet honey for all the nectar-eating birds. All the insects come for the honey too, and the many types of sugarbag or native bees are so happy, taking the pollen to their nesting areas. The long-nose sugarbag is the best one and he normally lives in the parent trees. There are thousands of old, scarred sugarbag ironwood trees scattered across many homelands across Australia. This is the evidence that the old people used to collect honey from many sugarbag nests, and there were plenty of them. Native honey was such an important food source for the people. Even all the ground flowering plants would produce their share of pollen for those living creatures that needed it. The insects that are attracted to the blooming plants then become important food sources for many other animals – insect-eating birds, lizards, possums, frogs and many more that depend on the healthy insect world to feed upon.

After the fire, the new fresh sweet green grass starts to shoot for many animals to graze on. Old, dead grass is no good for the animals; it is too hard for the animals' stomachs. Dry grass doesn't hold many nutrients for the grass-eating animals either. When the grass is ready to burn and it must burn, it ensures the grass seed can be produced every year at its best. Grass seed is another valuable prize that is produced from the vast varieties of grasses. Seed-eating bird species and other types of animals rely on the fresh grass seed cycles. Aboriginal people harvested many of the seeds to make flour for their range of cakes and breads. The burning of the grass in fire-dependent ecosystems is part of renewing the whole life cycle for those particular countries.

When country burns, it is lore to make sure not to burn the canopy of the trees. Poppy would always tell me that the canopy was sacred, another world that is above us and we must respect. It is the place where certain birds and other animals live, as it provides much-needed shade, shelter, water and food. Even the animals that live on the ground depend on the shade, food and medicines from the trees. The practice of burning to protect the trees come in respect of looking after all of the plants and animals.

Poppy would also say that we need to look after the trees to protect their totems that belonged to their people and themselves. All of the animals and plants are skin names, sacred, a totem to Aboriginal people today, and their ancestors. The trees play an important role for the people and have done for thousands of years. Looking after the trees and landscape meant looking after the animals and plants that were special to the people culturally. It is another level to cultural burning that connects people to the landscape in ways that adds more responsibility to look after the land properly. For Aboriginal people, a grandmother could have a totem from a certain bird, or a brother could have a goanna totem, and so on. It is another way in which people were one with the country and equal to each other through natural lore and spirituality.

The shade from the trees shares a role in creating a certain condition that combines with the rain, sun, dew, soils, and seasons to provide life. Many animals and people sleep in the shade on hot days. Kangaroos spend most of their time resting in the shade during the day. You don't see many of our land animals running around in the hot sun. They are resting in the shade until the cooler afternoons, evenings and mornings come to give them better conditions for their usual routines.

Certain trees were popular for the old people to set up camps under as well, keeping cool in the hotter times of the year. It's no doubt that the most important thing needed in a country with lots of sun is shade. Shade is as important as food and water, and it only makes sense to protect and respect the shade trees offer in every way possible. If the seasons get hotter then we need to ensure the trees are protected so that they can protect everything else. If we look after trees, we have a better chance of a long, sustainable life on Earth.

The trees were managed to stay on the country, to grow old and become the Elders of the landscape, maintaining their gift of providing life and prosperity for every other living thing within their environment. Aboriginal land management ensured that most of the trees lived to be hundreds or even a thousand years old. They populated the country in plenty, drawing and giving goodness to the ground to provide the essentials for a healthy landscape. The trees are so special, they are the lungs of our Earth. They are the providers of everything we need in more ways than anyone can imagine. They are the key to understanding how we apply fire to the landscape. If you don't know the trees then you will never know how to apply fire the way Aboriginal people have done to look after the land.

Part three

The other side

Chapter 10
The other side

Ten years goes by quite swiftly when you are having fun living such a lifestyle. But like living in any small town, there comes a time when you need a break for a while. So it was decided that it was time to leave Laura town for a little bit and see what the rest of the world was up to. The only problem was I didn't know where I was going to go, or what I was going to do. There wasn't any immediate reason for me to leave, I just had that good feeling that it was something I had to do. But out of the blue, of all places, I got offered a job working for the national parks.

It was the year 2001 and technology was well and truly on the rise. I never owned a mobile phone before, I never surfed the internet, and I never had an email account. Being in the bush had kept me away from those sorts of communications as I never had the need to use them. I was totally unskilled for a job in the mainstream at that time. I had no idea at all when it came to office work, or dealing with the government system. It was my childhood friend from Kuranda, Barry Hunter, who introduced me to this kind of world. He got me a job as a project officer in the Indigenous Unit of the Queensland Parks and Wildlife Service in Cairns. Yes, that's right, working for parks.

Barry was the team leader of the Indigenous Unit, whose purpose was to help Indigenous communities around Cape York and the Wet Tropics region. I stressed to him that I wasn't sure that I could do the job, due to my lack of government understanding and communication skills. He ensured me that I would be fine and encouraged me to move to

Cairns and try it out. After a bit of thought, I bit the bullet and decided that it was time to learn about the government world.

When I told old man TG and Poppy that I was going to leave, they looked down in disappointment. It was hard on them and myself to do such a move; we were happy just poking along with what we were doing. I assured them that I wasn't going to leave for good, and that I would be back to keep working with them. That made them feel better, but they didn't want me to leave. The day soon came where I said goodbye and drove out of Laura town with the old people and families waving behind me. Off I went along the dusty road with my little family and all our possessions on board our second-hand Toyota HiLux.

When I got to Cairns I realised what I had just done. I was now out of the bush and in the city, and I felt a great loss. Even though I knew Cairns, I had never actually lived there and instantly missed little Laura town. I knew I was starting another chapter of much-needed lessons for the journey.

My first day came to start the new job as a project officer and I was really nervous. I walked into the flash, air-conditioned, three-storey office with busy people rushing around everywhere. It was the first time I had to wear shoes and dress nice for work, which felt a little weird. I walked down the hall to find where I was to be stationed and became at ease once I found Barry. He welcomed me and showed me my desk and the computer I was to work on. Then he showed me how to do an email and I was on my way, beginning my first day as an Indigenous project officer. It was all a surreal experience because I wouldn't be there at all if it wasn't for Barry. He didn't even put me through the interview process, or maybe that was the way it worked back then.

The area my position covered was the Wujal Wujal region, which was in the Wet Tropics bordering lower Cape York. I was happy about that, because I knew a few Kuku Yalanji people from that area. I had to help them develop land and cultural management projects within the national park. That part was right up my alley and I couldn't wait to get up there into the community and get started. I was thinking that this national parks job wasn't so bad after all. I could see the potential for great things to happen for the communities and country, working in here.

I started to do the internal work and communications to set up my first field trip to Wujal Wujal. I had to talk to a couple of other managers that were above Barry to get things moving. There are a lot of boss mans to go through to get things done, and there is another boss man to go to again after that. Then there was also the main boss man, who came up from Brisbane every once in a while to visit everyone in the building.

The uncomfortable part of the job was walking down the hallways to the boss man's office. It was almost like a walk of shame sometimes as people stared at me while I walked along the corridors. One of the long-serving veterans of the force met me halfway and looked me up and down. 'So you're the new Indigenous worker, hey? Do you fellows do any work?' He then smartly walked away, not even interested in an answer from me. It was an uncomfortable feeling for me, walking around in that environment. Going to the boss man's office reminded me of going to the principal's office at school. But the thought of getting out onto Yalanji country was always a good motivator to help me through.

The day came when I finally got to drive a national parks car up to Wujal Wujal to start talking to the people. They were happy to see me as much I was to see them, and I explained what I was employed to do. They weren't too sure about me working for the national parks, but they were happy that I wasn't sure either. In no time we were out on country with the Elders, talking about their management aspirations. They went to sacred places where tourists were not supposed to go and discussed how they wanted it managed. That soon started the first task of creating a restricted access area for the Yalanji people. I went back to the office and spoke to the boss man and after a few weeks it got approved. I was stoked with the outcome for the people and was starting to enjoy myself; if I'm going to be kicking goals like this I'll be happy, I thought.

When I went back to Wujal Wujal, the Elders were in good spirits and we started looking at the next aspiration. They wanted to make other sacred places protected as well, to protect the country and people. One of the requests from the old ladies was to stop people walking up a particular mountain, which was a very sacred place for them. It was important not to disturb the mountain, which had been that way so long before settlement. It is important to realise that putting back the traditional lore on the land would create one law for everyone. Aboriginal and non-Indigenous Australians would both not be allowed at a particular place. No one would be able to go there. It would be an area where nature could be left alone, without disturbance, and would have cultural significance for everyone.

It makes sense to insert the original traditional lore of managing parts of the country to create one law for everyone to abide by. It means that we would have conservation areas in Australia that are managed by Aboriginal people in the same way for thousands of years. It would bring so much respect to Aboriginal people and give non-Indigenous people a better understanding of Aboriginal land and cultural management on the landscape. These places are also in the sea as much as on the land, so it would be great for all protected areas to be based on Aboriginal restricted places. It made so much more sense than having different laws for black and white Australians, as the Western law implements.

I took the new projects back to the office and started talking to the boss men about the steps to make it happen. I was so excited for the Yalanji people and how this could spearhead great opportunities for the future. We could also start doing this for Poppy and TG's country as well. They had plenty of sacred waterholes and wetlands that were important to be managed properly. I happily walked through the corridors of the national parks office, saying good morning to everyone. My head was held high and I was in a buzz for the work that lay ahead. That's when I got a message from one of the boss men to visit his office.

I knocked on his door with a smile and he signalled me to come in without offering me a seat. Straight off he started to deliver his prepared speech to me. 'Mate, from now on you are not allowed to go anywhere with any of our vehicles or do any projects unless we tell you to.'

'But what about the projects I'm working on with my position? We're getting lots of great, important work done.'

He just shrugged his shoulders and said, 'No, not even those.'

'But isn't my position to get Parks to work closer with the community?'

He just shrugged his shoulders again and said nothing, except there was a smirk was on his face. I asked him if there was any reason for this decision and he just shrugged again and said, 'That's just the way it is.'

I told him that it was unprofessional not to have a good reason to stop doing the work. Again he shrugged and simply said, 'You can resign if you want to. All you have to do is write a letter saying you're resigning in two weeks and all will be fine.'

I immediately saw red and said once again that he was unprofessional, in a raised voice. I couldn't help but swear at him to finish off the conversation and storm off to my desk. Everyone else in the Indigenous Unit sat there and said nothing. Instantly I knew that I had to leave. Barry had already resigned a few weeks earlier, so that didn't help with my motivation. I immediately wrote the letter and threw it on the boss man's desk. Without looking at me once he said, 'Thank you very much, see you later.' That was it, that was my path in learning my first lessons about government bureaucracy and working in national parks.

During this time, though, I was also learning how to apply for funding grants to continue the recording of traditional knowledge with the old people. I always knew that the government agency was not the place for me, so with the last two weeks left in Parks, I worked on getting back to my own dreams. I had written a submission earlier and freakishly, only a day after I resigned, I received a letter saying that I got the funding. I don't know how I did it, I just put it down to the spirits guiding me along.

When I wrote the submission I needed to have a legal body to administrate the grant. I ended up talking to a local Aboriginal corporation called Balkanu, which was an Aboriginal corporation advocating for Cape York. They said they would do it and in no time I was back into recording knowledge. The grant had enough money for me to give myself a small wage, buy a second-hand four-wheel drive from the corporation, and have a little left over to pay for bits of Poppy and old man TG's time here and there. I was really appreciative of the support, and it was good for the corporation's business to house such a project. They gave me a small space to set up the old computer and then I was on my way again, heading back to Laura town.

When I got back to Laura, the old people and families were happy to see me again. Soon we were on our way once more, going back on country, recording and getting into the fire. It was happy days again, only I was living between both worlds of the bush and the city. I was driving back and forth from Cairns to Laura to keep things moving, endless trips including to many other communities of the top end of Queensland.

Moving back to Laura would have been better, but the kids were well and truly into school and they were enjoying their new surroundings. The old people weren't too happy with me going back and forth from Cairns. But at least we were together working again, and out bush doing what we have always done in our time together. Being on country and getting the fires going.

Chapter 11
The battle for acknowledgement

Things were going well, I was getting to spend plenty of time with Poppy and old TG again, as we continued our work from where we had left off. Things were almost back to normal with us on country. It was about this time I met a lady by the name of Peta Standley, Pete for short. She had a love for the environment and her heart was close to helping Aboriginal people in land management. She had worked with Indigenous communities before and was interested in what we were doing. She had more experience than me in negotiating with government agencies, which was the help we needed. With Pete and the recent native title land hand-back process, we were getting closer to burning more freely on Awu-Laya country.

More meetings followed, one after the other, to try and convince government agencies to allow the old people to burn their country. Then, eventually, we finally managed to get a fire permit for Poppy and TG and that was a big thing. The condition was we were only allowed to burn around Saxby Waterhole. Saxby is culturally special to the old people and they were stoked to finally start managing it on behalf of their ancestors. Poppy was so happy, he was burning freely without a care, and it was good to watch. As long as we stayed close to Saxby Waterhole, we were okay.

Awu-Laya country is located on a restricted section of the national

73

park, so the country was closed to public access. The only way in was through rough, unformed bush roads that ran through the cattle properties. So when we did our burning we were pretty much on our own and rarely saw anyone else. It was so relaxing, watching Poppy burn around the lagoon so gently, and then cast his rod and lure in the water to snag a barramundi. The old fellas got so comfortable that they started applying fire a little further into their country each time. Just sticking to Saxby Waterhole was not enough for them, so we started to burn around other story places in the area. Once they started looking after one place, they couldn't stop because the country needed it so bad. We wasn't supposed to, but no one really said anything because we were still on the land handed back to the old people.

After a couple of years the country was starting to look really good in many places. The native grasses were coming back stronger and healthier. The parts of country that were taken over by tea-tree were thinning out. The weeds were dying away and being replaced by a sea of native grasses, herbs and young, upcoming parent trees. As the country improved the two Elders, Poppy and TG, became more and more active and it made them happy. They had the country to themselves, a whole playground of introducing fire back onto the landscape. It was all the old people wanted, to have their land back again.

We would still get complaints and hear rumours every now and again, but it wasn't enough to stop us from what we were doing. The local land council assured us that it was the right of Aboriginal people to conduct their cultural practices under the *Aboriginal Land Act*. That seemed like a pretty good safeguard, so we took their advice and kept on burning country. Within no time we were starting to burn in many places on Awu-Laya country, but not all the places desired by the Elders. Much of their country was still on pastoral tenure and other areas were national park. They were also concerned for the neighbouring country that belonged to related clan groups in the area.

In some places the first fires we lit were a little hotter than normal, because there was so much dead grass and fuel. The old fellas didn't like to see heavy fuel loads and they would try and burn them if they could. Because of the large fuel loads of dead grass and weeds, the fires were producing a lot of smoke – more smoke than a healthy landscape would produce. We were also burning masses of invasive tea-tree that had started taking over the country after previous wildfires and other management burns. When we were treating the invasive tea-tree in ecosystems where they didn't belong, they would set off a much darker smoke than normal. But after the first burns the fires got smaller and the smoke became whiter and lighter. We could now drive to places on the country that the old men hadn't been to since they were young cattlemen roaming through on horseback. This allowed them to find more special cultural places, it was like they were unwrapping a big present. The joy it brought when they finally got to walk into these places after so long.

A few days later I was approached by Peta Standley with an offer for her to do a PhD based on the fire work we were doing. I wasn't too sure about that academic world as it didn't really work for me. I didn't even know what it took to write a PhD. The other part of my concern was that I didn't trust the Western system with such important knowledge. But with Pete and a few others educating me about the matter, I started to see that it might be a good idea. I came to thinking that it might help get the old people recognised. It could also help make it easier for the old fellas to get more freedom to burn on their country.

Then came the thought of not being sure about a white person being the author of a PhD about the old fellas' knowledge. She responded that she could apply to make them the authors as well. That meant she would be writing it for them, and they would be acknowledged to be the owners of the PhD and all of its contents. I knew that this was going to heavily involve me as well, so I had to think long and hard about it. Bringing Pete along to all our burns on country was a big commitment. In the end I said that I would support it only if the old people got their doctorates up-front. That they became recognised as doctors before the PhD even started. She looked very unsure about that, but then her attitude was, 'Why not? We can always try.'

That sounded pretty good to me, so we went to the old fellas to explain the project. Of course, they didn't understand that world either, but they thought that it might be a good way to get things moving. Old TG was really keen because he really knew and understood the word 'report'. He knew that the police did reports, and that national parks rangers did reports, and on a few occasions I witnessed him watching the newsman on the television reading reports. 'Look, boy, that fella is reading the report. He's going to get things going for us.' I would always chuckle to myself at those moments and I would usually say, 'We won't get help from that fella, old man.' He would always argue the case though, trying to convince me by pointing his pipe at the television screen. 'You listen, boy.'

When it came to communicating the idea of the PhD, we made sure that everyone understood the whole process and what it meant for the whole clan. After all the talks with the Elders and their families about it, everyone was in favour. Everyone seemed to get along with Pete as well, and the Elders enjoyed working with her too. The family felt safe about the project as I was directly involved, trusting that it would be done the right way. Having the trust of everyone was certainly why the idea became a reality. But most importantly, everyone could see that this was the old people's dream, to have their country back culturally. It was a way to recognise their knowledge, their hard work and passion.

Finally I could see how the old fellas' PhD process could hopefully set a different example in supporting Indigenous knowledge. One where the knowledge keeper is the owner and is acknowledged properly. Where the process empowers Elders' aspirations. Meanwhile, Pete told me about the process of getting the Elders their doctorates up-front through James Cook University in Cairns. This was also the university where she would base the PhD. She informed the university on what we wanted to do, knowing that it wasn't going to be easy. Universities just don't give away doctorates to anyone that asks, at the best of times. But she managed to get the idea presented to the university committee all the same.

We started the long process of contacting key academic people who had involved the old people in their research in the past. We asked them to send letters of support for the process so we could add them to the argument. To explain how these academics became doctors with the help of the Elders and their knowledge. We mentioned the current traditional knowledge recording work the Elders were doing – that was good credit for the cause too.

The whole process took a long time as the committee meetings were spaced far apart. They needed to dwell on the proposal for a while, and we kept gathering more supporting documents to convince them along the way. The day did eventually come when we heard the good news, and what a wonderful thing to happen for the Elders. The date was set for 13 May 2005 for them to officially become doctors. The whole process took a long twelve months, but in the end it was well worth the happy ending. To tell you the truth, I never thought it would happen, but it did.

The day they graduated was no doubt a special day. They were so proud, dressed up in their funny blue medieval-looking doctorate suits. We all had a chuckle seeing them there in that kind of dress. That floppy hat hanging off their heads like they were a pair of black Picassos. But their glowing faces and big smiles just took over the whole look. They got their photos taken many times and had media grab them for quick interviews to feed a number of newspaper articles. The old fellas were becoming recognised through all their work and I couldn't be prouder with the outcome. The day continued on with food and celebration at the local park in Cairns. I couldn't help but play some music with some local musicians. It was a time to celebrate the old people, a day of recognising their knowledge and contribution. It was a historic day, and in the end we had proudly announced Dr George Musgrave and Dr Tommy George.

After all the excitement from the doctorate ceremony, we were motivated more than ever to manage country with fire. Having Pete around doing the PhD pushed us to seek new areas to trial the burns. We needed to go to different places to cover all the types of country and situations. Poppy was also keen to burn different areas of the park other than Thaypan country. He was related through kin to the neighbouring clan group Elders and they would come out too on occasion in support. The other reason he wanted to venture elsewhere was to visit old secret fishing spots. There were always other important reasons to burn in the other areas. Poppy started rattling off a few names of places where he would like to burn and we noted them down.

I knew that it wasn't going to be easy to break it to national parks, but we had to give it a go. We ventured out to the areas where the Elders wanted to burn so that we could see what the country looked like and plan our approach. When we got out there we ran into a couple of the local rangers standing next to their cars, a little off the road. They were there looking at a tourist site that they were working on in the park. We pulled over next to them to give them a greeting and tell them what we were up to. Poppy was always first to say hello with his high, happy voice and cheeky laugh.

The rangers greeted us in return and then we started a general goodwill conversation. 'So what are you doing out here, old fella? Going fishing?', the ranger said. Poppy and the ranger exchanged a bit more chit-chat and then Poppy ended up mentioning burning country. I asked the ranger about doing some burns in other places in the park. Poppy instantly responded, asking the ranger if we could light some fires. The ranger replied, 'You want to light some fires? Yeah, no worries, you can light some fires.' He then reached through his car window, pulled out a box of matches and threw them at Poppy. 'Here you are, old fella, knock yourself out.'

As he was saying those words Poppy caught the flying box of matches with one hand from the passenger window. We looked at each other in disbelief of what had just happened. I had to double-check, so I asked the ranger again if we could burn. He replied once again that it was okay for us to go ahead. 'Alright, we gonna go now', yelled Poppy with his little giggle and without another moment wasted he gave me the sign to drive on. Old TG was sitting in the middle and let out a short, sharp laugh of happiness as he puffed on his pipe with approval. 'That's good, they gotta work with us. They're listening to us now.'

We drove off happy as anything, waving to the ranger as we sped off down the dirt road in search of our destination. That day we burnt the areas the old men wanted to and they were beautiful burns. Poppy walking through the country with his piece of burning paperbark, appearing and disappearing in and out of the trees. Putting the fire in all the right places as he walked through the landscape. You could see old TG sitting on a log reloading his pipe as he watched the beauty unfold. I could see great things coming from all of this, now that the rangers were onside. It must have been the old people getting their doctorates that changed their ways, or maybe the PhD project. Either way, I was looking forward to working with them further in getting things going with Indigenous fire management in Rinyirru (Lakefield) National Park.

The next day we were home again only to receive a slightly different message from the park rangers. We were told that we could not do any more burns unless we informed them first and got a permit. I didn't know where that came from, but we were okay with that and agreed that it was fair enough. We did tell the ranger that we wanted to burn and he said it was okay to do so. We wanted to do the right thing by them as well, so we responded, saying we'd like to meet to discuss our next plans.

We had to painfully go through numerous meetings to gain permissions and it wasn't just with the local ranger. We had to meet with the head managers in the Cairns office as well, just for a fire permit. It became a huge, complicated process and the attitude was the total opposite to how that ranger acted that day. What was that ranger thinking when he threw that box of matches at us, talking like that? He must have thought that we wouldn't do it, that we were too lazy or something. I think he realises now that he threw that box of matches at the wrong people.

After all the negotiations we managed to get a permit to burn some new country on the park, and it was great. It was our first permit in the form of a piece of paper and it was a pretty special moment. I showed the old people the permit and we all admired it like it was a letter from the Queen herself. We were happy and it felt like we were getting somewhere once again. On the day of the burn I picked up the Elders for the journey. We also had Pete come along for another day in the field with us. We drove about a half an hour down the dusty road until we got close to the national park boundary fence. As we got closer, we saw what looked like a four-wheel drive parked halfway across the road. At first we thought someone might be having car trouble, but as we got closer we noticed that it was a national parks vehicle. Standing in front of the vehicle was a ranger in full uniform, waving at us to stop.

We had never seen this fella around before, so we were quite confused as to what was going on. His socks were pulled up high, shirt tucked in, pen and notepad in his top pocket, and a flat-brimmed hat to boot. It looked like it was his first day on the job 'cause he looked real flash. We pulled over and I greeted him by asking if everything was alright. He told us that they had suddenly decided to cancel our permit and not let us burn. I couldn't believe what I was hearing, and why did they send this new stranger ranger to tell us at the very last minute? 'But we have already had meetings with the head staff about this,' I said back, pulling the permit out of the glove box to show the man. He didn't even look at the wrinkled, now-worthless piece of paper. Instead, he just stood there shaking his head in disapproval. I asked him why he was doing this. He looked at me with a smirky grin on his face and mumbled, 'I don't know, it's just the way it is.'

That kind of answer made me furious and I could see the same anger in the eyes of the old men. Being that I was young and hot-headed at the time, I continued to argue with the ranger. He just stood there, saying nothing but shaking his head and shining his bleak smile of authority at us. That only made me more wild, which triggered off the harsher words in the argument. Then Poppy muffled a few words to me – 'Don't worry about him' – and gave me that familiar hand sign to drive on. I quickly finished off my last say and drove off, proceeding into the national park as ordered by my mentors.

As we continued down the road we were all a bit stunned about what just happened, but we were all angry as hell. The boss man had once again put the old people in their place, except this time the Elders weren't impressed. I was really disappointed that we couldn't burn and knew that it was way out of the question. So I made a joke and said that we should just go ahead and burn anyway. Poppy answered back quickly, saying, 'Yeah, alright, go ahead.' I laughed, thinking that the old man was playing along with my wild suggestion. But when I looked at him, he was dead serious and he wasn't smiling. Old man TG was muffling strong words through his pipe and giving hand signs of approval to burn the country. 'Bugger them, we've done everything the right way.' Old TG went on to say that he was the boss, not the ranger, pointing to his own Aboriginal ranger badge on his shoulder sleeve.

Hearing those old men talk like this lit me up with confidence and I could see that they were in war mode. Pete was in the back, enjoying the whole show, jotting things down for her PhD as we went along. From there we started to look for places to burn, and burn we did. We lit many places that day in different areas of the park. We would hit one place and then take off to the next place to try and manage as much country as we could. They were beautiful fires, each one lit up in the right place, burning only where we wanted it to burn. It felt like we were noble bandits, running around trying to look after the land. At one point I looked back and saw puffs of white smoke here and there in the distance. From where I was standing it was a wonderful sight to see, but I figured that wouldn't be a nice view from the local ranger base.

Of course I knew our fires were not going to go down well with the authorities, but the fight had gone on for too long. I did think about what they might do in response, which made me feel a little bit nervous. But the orders from the Elders are way more powerful than the orders from any Western authority in my books. So I reassured myself that everything would be fine and we kept on driving around, burning country.

The next day I got the phone call as expected from the head office in Cairns. The local rangers were not talking to us now, which left us with the tablecloth shirt boss on our case. The tablecloth shirt boss is the main district boss of all the little boss men. (It's those checked, button-up dress shirts that have that tablecloth design on them.) 'We can take you to court for what you did. That's considered arson,' he said to me. I replied to him that court was a good idea and that it would be good if we can all put everything on the table. I went on to ask him about the process in taking us to court and how we could help make it happen. Without another word he hung up and I never heard from them again about that incident. The only thing that came through the grapevine was tall stories and whispers. Some said we lit the whole park up, but that didn't worry me because there was no hot fires for them to carry on. The rumours of those times still make sure my name is not a favourable one for fire management in their domain.

From there things didn't go too well in our relationship with the national parks and more heated moments would arise here and there. Then incidents occurred like getting blamed for a wildfire that burned through the park and went into the neighbouring cattle property. There was no way we would have lit that fire because I was in Cairns at the time and we would never burn country at that time of year. As a result I started getting threatening calls from a random station owner and he left some pretty bad messages for me.

When the old people found out, they were so angry that they went out to inspect where the fire came from. They were trackers, so that is a pretty easy task for them to do. They found the point where the fire started, but who knows who might have been responsible. Old man TG was affected the most. He even went down to the police station to tell them what had happened. Of course, the coppers shrugged their shoulders and never took up the complaint from the old man. It didn't stop old man TG stomping around the community talking about it for a few days.

It was such a shame that our relationship with the national parks was over, because we tried hard on many accounts to get them involved. But every time we got the chance to interpret the landscape to them from the traditional perspective, it fell on deaf ears. They were so intimidated to hear anything that we tried to tell them about the country. Whenever we showed them the indicators of sick country, they would take it personally, maybe because they were the managers? It was the perfect example of the ignorant attitudes we were facing.

Either way, I didn't care anymore and I let go to give myself peace of mind. I had given up on trying to change things by having meetings with the government. It wasn't doing the people or country any good and it certainly wasn't working in favour of the PhD project. It didn't do national parks any good either, because in the end it gets no one anywhere. So from there I pulled back a bit and asked the Elders if we could focus on just burning the land around Saxby and lay low for a little while. I figured that we could do more burns peacefully, without going through so much trouble.

Time was too precious to waste on pointless government meetings, especially with the Elders getting older. We were still doing traditional knowledge work here and there with other communities as well. It's a shame to say but when it came to the Aboriginal aspirations of looking after country and reviving our culture, the government just got in the way. They forced us to try and avoid them as much as possible; so sad that nothing positive came from trying to involve them. So go back to Saxby is what we did, and from there we had another couple of amazing years burning out on Awu-Laya country.

But the whole process of locking horns with national parks wasn't all wasted. I learnt a lot of lessons and it did help me steer the work into a more sensible direction. A direction where more fun and time on the land was had with the people from the land. As a result, we did so much good work that we also helped inspire other communities. But I still had hope that one day the Western world would help us and become a part of the process.

Chapter 12

The obstacle of man

Based on my experiences, the hardest thing to deal with when putting Aboriginal fire management onto the landscape is people. It's straightforward to get out there and start managing the land, but too often people seem to get in the way, regardless of who they are or whom they represent. But let me get one thing straight before you continue to read this very difficult but important chapter: I have much respect for modern humanity. It's just that so many people are separated not only from the land, but also from each other.

It seems that many people don't understand certain knowledge values that come from our ancient cultures of the earth, and this absence has created a majority of humans who are unconscious of the natural world we live in. When you really think about it, it seems so dangerous to have the majority of mankind heading in a direction where they are disconnected from the land.

It is now time to start educating our massive disconnected population to change their ways, now that critical environmental disasters are starting to occur. How do we get people to shift their ways and create change that is going to lead us to the solutions we need? It's like we need to reset and decolonise our society to make us in tune with our Mother and each other. No doubt there will be values to adopt from all Indigenous knowledge systems, which can be joined together with Western influence to help guide us along on a safer road. If this is going to happen, then it might pay to go back a few steps to regain what was lost in the past. To get people on the same page and in sync, with the same respect and understanding of the adaptation needed ahead. So far, based my own experiences, it does seem possible, but what a hell of a mess we need to start working through.

As we all know, there are so many views of the world that are mainly based on human interest and not the land. When it comes to understanding natural concepts like fire alone, it is so often misunderstood. And there are many communities and government agencies that don't work together. Implementing Aboriginal fire knowledge into a society like this comes with so many challenges.

You have to deal with politicians, government workers, rural fire agencies, forestry, corporates, councils, scientists, universities, national parks, greenies, private landholders, not to mention people in general, who are either terrified of fire or just don't care at all. Overall, the Western vision of fire is all about life, property, fear and fighting fire. If it is not about that, then it's suppressing fire from the land altogether, thinking it's entirely bad for the environment. As a result, we have ended up with disharmony, in terms of the different mindsets within our society, and in our country.

One time I was invited to attend and speak at an international fire conference in a capital city. The venue was a huge building in the CBD and hundreds of delegates were walking around wearing name tags. There were presentation rooms everywhere, including one massive hall full of displays and stalls. I soon realised that it was a big showroom representing the fire culture of the modern world. There were big fire trucks and all kinds of the latest firefighting equipment out for display and on offer. It was good to see that they had so much safety equipment to assist in aiding disasters, that was for sure.

I wanted to see what else they had in that massive room that was of interest to me. I set off to take my own personal tour of what was going on. I got about three stalls through when a guy walked over to greet me. 'Hey, take one of these empty shopping bags and fill it up with all the merchandise you can find. There's free hats, pens, t-shirts, and if you're quick, you can even get oven mitts made from the latest fireproof material.' I took the bag and thanked him as I walked down the aisles to check it all out.

As I browsed along, I met a happy man with a big come-to-my-shop smile on his face. 'Come and have a look at this', he said. He showed me what he called a fireproof guttering system for your house. If that wasn't good enough, then you could buy a bunker for your backyard. 'All you have to do is run into the bunker and you'll be safe from the fire.' I asked him a few questions about the features out of interest and we broke into a small conversation.

He saw that I didn't have a name tag and asked what brought me to the conference. I told him I did Indigenous fire management and he paused for a moment. He soon ended the conversation, slowly walking away, saying, 'That's wonderful, you have a nice day.' It was clear that my occupation was of no interest in his world. Out of all the stalls there was nothing that represented Indigenous fire management, or looking after the land. No doubt we need the firefighting equipment to fight fires and save lives and property, but we also need to look after the land too. Why isn't the subject of prevention and proactive measures being shared too?

Moments later the keynote speaker started his speech in the main presentation room. There was a massive crowd sitting down listening in awe of what he was saying. He sensitively displayed a graph tallying up the destruction of the recent fires of that time. His speech assured the audience that improved evacuation plans were in place and better firefighting equipment was on the way. Everything was based on fighting fire, safety, and selling the fear to each and every one. It made me feel quite strange and out of place, like I was on another planet. I was observing a culture that had become completely oblivious to the land. With all of this going on around me I realised that the firefighting industry must be worth a lot of money.

A change in mindset is made even harder with government processes and laws being completely out of sync with natural lore. Many government-funded programs are so off the mark simply because the financial reporting dates steer the ship more than nature. Looking

Victor recording Poppy as he talks about a healthy patch of wild rice

Dr George Musgrave and Dr Tommy George at their Honorary Doctorate ceremony

Dale and Lewis Musgrave taking over from their grandfathers

Dr Tommy George conducting a burn in boxwood country

A fire workshop conducted for communities in southern Queensland

Dr George Musgrave and Dr Tommy George holding a fire torch

Dr George Musgrave's grandson, Lewis Musgrave, conducting the usual burn

Victor Steffensen attending a fire workshop in Bega, New South Wales

after the country with fire is a commitment that goes on forever into the future; it's not a program that is funded for three to five years and then stops. You can't have people burning country to funding guidelines rather than the right time for the country.

Every year I get calls from people that want to burn at that same time when their financials are due. Many are trying to burn country that is not ready at that particular time of year. I tell them no, you can't burn that country now. But some are persistent and want to make it happen so they can report and get the next round of funding. They have to spend the money and finish the project before a set date.

Getting the green light from government officials to do cultural burns is another challenge. One time I was helping a community to get their first cultural fire happening on their country. The Aboriginal-owned land had rangers and Elders working on the property for three days, planning for the burn. They also had a good relationship with the neighbouring farmer and the local fire brigade officer, so they were there learning too, and fully onside to get the burns happening. We walked all over the property, going through all the knowledge indicators and preparing to light the grass. As usual I was helping the community to film a fire assessment for their project.

They were so eager to learn and were emotionally excited by the idea of burning on their own country. Everything was set up ready to go, the permits were set, the local fire officer was on-site. There were six Aboriginal rangers, two slip-on firefighting units, radios, firebreaks, and the neighbour was there with smiles from ear to ear. All they had to do now was telephone the authorities in the capital city five hundred kilometres away to let them know. I sat down in the dry grass and had a rest while they made the call to light up.

It wasn't long before I noticed the Elders looking pretty disturbed as they walked around aimlessly, shaking their heads. I got up and walked over to see what was wrong. 'They won't let us burn,' the old man said in a real disappointed voice. 'The guy far away isn't happy with our firebreaks and thinks we haven't done a good enough job.' The old man made me feel sorry and I could see the hurt in his eyes. It was a look that said he had dealt with this kind of hurt many times before. How can they make fire management decisions for the land by sitting in an office looking at maps?

I couldn't help but ask the old man the ultimate question. 'Old fella, do you want to burn or don't you want to burn?' He looked up at me and said, 'I want to burn.' 'Well, let's burn then', I said. He nodded with a cheeky smile and then yelled out to the team to saddle up. The local fire officer smiled and then shrugged his shoulders in agreement. 'I'm just gonna pretend that I'm not here at all.' Everyone laughed and was happy again as they gathered round in excitement for a prep talk. I suggested that we burn at night so that people wouldn't see the smoke and call it in. It would be cooler too, which would be good because of all the fuel that was choking up the country. They all agreed and that night we had a beautiful burn that went out at one o'clock in the morning. The fire had burned cool through the night and treated the area that we intended to clean up without anyone noticing.

The next day was followed by the Elders proudly watching the young rangers continuing their film assessment of the burnt country. I wouldn't have agreed to burn if it was the wrong time of the year, with extreme weather conditions. But the main reasons to burn were because it was the right time and we had the local community there. Black and white working together, with all the right procedures in place. Sometimes you just have to bite the bullet and let commonsense prevail. Especially if the whole community is there working together in support of each other. What can the boss man do if the community stands strong together?

Don't get me wrong – there are many good people of all nationalities working for government agencies that are trying to help the community. Many of them are trying to work from the inside to change things and many are passionate too. If they were not there it would be a lot harder to get most things happening at all. We certainly need good brothers and sisters of all bloodlines in those positions. But on many occasions I've seen them pull their hair out trying, or giving up altogether, from this constant uphill battle with the system.

One time I was working in a region down south to get the first burns happening on country. We did workshops over and over for three years, trying to get to the point of conducting a cultural burn. On every occasion the boss man from the lower ranks kept putting safety excuses in the way. All we wanted to do was one little demonstration site to show them the burning techniques.

But regardless of not putting fire on the ground, three years of workshops got many people within the agency interested. Eventually the main regional boss decided to turn up and within the first hour he approved the burn with the click of his fingers. After three years of excuses for why we shouldn't burn, this big boss of all the little bosses made it happen instantly. I stood there and looked at the little boss men in silence for a moment or two in disbelief. 'Why couldn't you get this fella out here in the first place, instead of three years of time, energy and money wasted?'

When I was younger I was a lot less experienced in delivering the Indigenous knowledge perspective without offending certain people. I do admit to being a little hot-headed in the earlier days, not that it wasn't needed on occasions in those times. I've now grown to deliver the message more gently, because getting angry doesn't work. It is hard being in the position to deliver these views to so many mindsets, but it's important to be patient and allow for the understanding of others. The message needs to come across clearly and represented as accurately as possible, with the community taking the lead on their own country.

One day I went to look at some country with a crew of Aboriginal national park rangers who are cultural burners. I jumped in the car with them and we headed off to our destination. As always they were cheerful and showing willingness to learn. They told me that the main boss ranger, who was non-Indigenous, was waiting up the road to meet us and join us for the day. 'No worries', I told them, and before long we were pulling up to a man standing with his arms crossed waiting for our arrival.

I jumped out of the car and walked over to him with a smile and my hand extended out for that traditional greeting. 'Hi, how are you going?' I said. He quickly cut me off and said, 'Before you say anything else I want to tell you that there is nothing you can tell me about fire. I've been doing burning for over twenty years.' I got a bit of a shock and slowed my greeting walk to a standstill. 'Okay, let's go then', I said, trying to keep positive. He told me to leave my car behind and jump in with him.

The other boys jumped in too and I made my way to the back seat window to settle in for the short journey. As we drove I couldn't see very much healthy country along the way. I broke the silence and asked him where we were going. 'I'm going to take you up to where we just did a burn recently.' Up the road we went until I saw what looked like burnt country. It was a tall stringybark forest and the tree canopies were wilted, with dead brown leaves.

As we got out of the car and walked towards the site the Aboriginal rangers were trying to whisper to me, 'Look at the trees, they are all burnt.' The Aboriginal rangers had already been to a few fire workshops and their observations were in line with what I was seeing. When we got to the burnt, blackened forest, I positioned everyone a few metres in to make an assessment. The rangers looked a bit nervous as they waited for me to start talking about the poor country.

I took a breath and thought a bit on how I could say what I was seeing in the nicest way possible. 'I want you to know that what I'm about to say is just what I see from the lens of Indigenous knowledge. I don't want you to get offended in any way. I'm not trying to criticise you or say you're doing things wrong.' The boss man nodded his head and straightened himself up to listen.

I pointed out that the timing and frequency for the stringybark country didn't look right due to the state of the forest. You could see that everything on the ground was burnt black as a cinder and there was nothing left. When you burn stringybark country properly, it is a gentle fire, and there should still be some medicinal and food plants left still green. There must have been way too much fuel in there for the fire to burn like that. The fire before that must have also been hot and burned for much longer. The trees were burnt black and the canopy was all dead, which made the sun get through too much. I then pointed out that the fires were lit from the bottom of the hill and done in a drip torch fashion. The silence and absence of anything living or foraging in the damaged ecosystem was also shared among the group.

The boss man took it all in and then said that it wasn't his burn because he wasn't there when it happened. Instead he now stated that it was his staff that undertook the burn and not himself.

One thing I'd love to see is for the government to effectively jump in the passenger seat and let us drive for a change. Being in the passenger seat means that they are still in the same car, so we won't leave them behind. But most of the time we are not even in the car and they just drive off, leaving us in the dust. We watch the car zoom off down the road and then we see it pull over in the far distance, breaking down. We sit in the dust and wait patiently for them to come back and pick us up.

One time I was helping Traditional Owners to prepare for a major fire workshop event. We decided we wanted to burn a little bit of country close to camp, to clean up a bit and set the scene. Because we were holding the workshop on a national park the head fire ranger was involved in the logistics. They were totally nervous and it was understandable, because of some recent bushfires in the region.

We told the head ranger what we wanted to do and the boss man responded that we could only burn one square metre here and there. Come again, one square metre? The idea was to dig a square metre break in the dirt and then burn the leaf litter in the middle. We had to laugh about this request, because it was funny. When the ranger left, one of the brothers from that country was ready to start burning, but a little confused. 'How are we supposed to burn country like that, walking around digging a square metre everywhere?'

We could see that the fire couldn't go anywhere as there were natural firebreaks of bare dirt everywhere throughout the sickened landscape. It was the right time to burn too, so we didn't have any worries. We couldn't stick to the square metre policy – that just goes against the essence of traditional fire knowledge. The brother from that country lit the messy layer of leaf litter and we watched it ever so slowly trickle along in a peaceful way. He had to walk around and burn other patches to ensure the fire could travel as it needed to. I continued working on other stuff around the camp, watching him caretaking the little clean-up burns from afar.

The tiny fires went out that very afternoon and left a mosaic of burnt patches of land here and there. By next morning many people were arriving and the excitement was starting to travel through the air. I stood with some of the Traditional Owners and event managers, talking on the plans. It was at that moment that the parks staff rolled up in a few vehicles and parked across the road next to the burnt areas. We watched them walk into the burnt country and gather round to discuss what they were witnessing. It was like watching a football team gather round to do a prep talk before running on the field. Then finally they broke up and their star players started their long but short walk over to where we were standing.

'Good morning,' we all said as they walked within the acknowledgement space for a greeting. 'How are you all going?' The boss man started off by saying that everything looked so great with the workshop set-up, but they only had one problem. 'What could that be?' we all responded. 'We're not happy that you're burning out of the one-square-metre requirements and not within the proposed burn zone.' The head ranger then went on to say that we needed to talk about this immediately. I suggested that we all went over into the burnt country to discuss the matter, so we could be in the place of question. There was a good representation of Traditional Owners, organisers and park staff there to begin the session.

To cut a long conversation short, we explained that burning involves identifying what needs to burn from a traditional knowledge perspective. Going on from there we told the ranger that the minute you apply Western management concepts, it is no longer an Indigenous fire workshop. It goes against the logic and the traditional form of the practices altogether. People who come to learn will not experience the value of the knowledge or see it demonstrated.

They all understood clearly what we were saying and I could see a more relaxed acceptance shine through their faces. Our discussion ended with a lot more confidence in the ability for us to do what we had to do. It wasn't entirely perfect to our vision, but at least we could demonstrate freely on the ground we had. 'Okay, let's go and kick this workshop off,' I encouraged, clapping my hands together to everyone. The boss man stopped me and said that there was one more thing to tell me that I wasn't going to like. 'Victor, you can't go on the fire ground with the Crocs shoes that you're wearing, I'm really sorry.'

'But these are the shoes I have been wearing at every fire around the country since I've been burning away from home,' I said to the ranger, in the nicest way possible. I won't wear the safety gear, no matter how hard they try to make me. I can't wear the big boots because I can't feel the country, and I trip all the time. The only time I'll wear them is if I'm walking in the snow in minus-degree temperatures. If the old people could see me wearing full PPE (personal protective equipment) at a fire they would giggle and look at me funny. It goes against everything they have ever taught me, because it just isn't a part of our world. Maybe we can make sure all the participants have the helmets and stuff on, but I just can't do it.

The boss man continued to apologise but stood his ground, saying that I was not allowed to enter the fire zone. 'What do we need to do to fix this?', I responded in a creative way. 'Maybe you can write a little letter stating that you sign the liability over to me instead of your agency.' He thought about it for a few seconds and then agreed that it was a good idea. He pulled out a notepad and started writing on the bonnet of a four-wheel drive. I was surprised because I didn't think he would take me seriously on that request. 'Here you go – sign right here at the bottom.'

I took the pen and signed and that was that, I was able to do my thing the way I have always done. The ranger seemed relieved once we made the transaction, and stated that we should make a template of the agreement for future situations. It was the first time that this had actually happened to me and it created happiness between us. It wasn't long after that that the safety concerns settled right down as they realised the situation was calm and everybody was safe. The whole workshop was magical with about five hundred people enjoying the magic of learning on country together.

By the last day the boss man was looking so happy, you could see the real person inside coming out. He came up to me exclaiming that it was such a lovely event, 'amazing' in his words. Then said that he realised how structured by the system he was and that it was a load off his shoulders. His face was lit up, he was free from a side of himself that was deprived of the truth and the freedom that comes from the land. I was happy for him and for the others too that were a part of the crew. I could see the happiness in them too as they smiled in all four directions. It was a beautiful moment and everyone felt the love.

Don't let this story make you think that we don't need safety gear – I don't want anyone to think that. But the safest thing you can have on country when burning is knowledge. If that is activated then we can relax a little more and enjoy so many more benefits. That's why we need to see more workshops on country, and government agencies supporting community-led initiatives instead of running them. There have been government Indigenous fire programs dressing up Aboriginal people with full safety gear and a drip torch, then teaching them how to burn the Western way and calling it cultural burning. It is not a good feeling for Aboriginal people, and it takes away the chance to revive many of the values.

I can attest to the fact that Aboriginal people are a sharing and caring race with values that are not based on fear, domination and greed. The old people told me that when a tribe of people sat around the fire to eat, they would give everyone a piece each. Share the same amount and make sure that everyone had their fill. When I sit with the homeless that live on the streets, they will share their last dollar with me and offer the last drop of wine. We will let the white fella ride in our car, even if they made us walk all the way most of the time. No matter what they do to the people and the country, most Aboriginal people want to help, because it is a beautiful part of the resilience within all Indigenous cultures.

And in spite of so many mindsets and so many problems, the truth is these things have strengthened my methods and have made my spirit stronger. I can honestly say that it has made me a better person from where I started from, that is for sure. Nobody is perfect, that is so true, and we can all overcome the illnesses that lurk deep within. Forgiveness is also important because people just don't know. But once they step foot on country, accompanied with timeless knowledge and understanding, the healing begins.

Chapter 13
Science or oppression?

I remember one adventure in the earlier days, I was filming Poppy talking about traditional food lores and diet. Even all the different foods had different lore for each stage of a person's life. Depending on your age, gender or totem, the food lores were there to avoid complications and sickness. The people were always eating foods that were in season, which is actually the healthiest way you can eat. Only eating what the universe provides, at the right time it is ready. Poppy and old TG were always rattling off the food lores and, as always, I listened and learnt. It was serious business and it was always strictly abided by in the old times.

Somehow Poppy got onto the topic of what pregnant women should eat within Awu-Laya lore. In his way, it's the man's job to know what food to get for his wife. Poppy started rattling off heaps of different foods of what can and can't be eaten. 'They can eat the sugarbag honey, plants and little animals, things like that, but they can't eat big fish or goanna, turtle, things like that'. There is always a sacrifice to help go through different phases in life and as he went on, it made a lot of sense. 'After the baby is born, she'll be right then, she can eat anything she likes, she'll be happy.' Poppy gave off that high-pitched laugh once more as we signed off for the day.

That late afternoon I started a four-hour drive to Cairns, thinking about what we had discussed. I turned on the car radio and tuned into the ABC station for something to listen to. Ironically, it was an interview of a scientist talking about how pregnant women shouldn't eat certain fish. He said that the mercury in the fish is bad for pregnant women and that it could cause difficulties for their babies. The scientist was basically talking about the same thing we recorded out in the bush that day. The old people knew that knowledge through their food lores developed over thousands of years.

Throughout the earlier years of living in Laura, right through to the present day, I have seen many researchers come and go. All sorts of strangers from different universities would come and interview the Elders on whatever topic they were after, sometimes offering the old people a few hundred bucks, or most times nothing at all. They would go away with the information and then we'd never hear from most of them again. I remember times in the early 1990s when scientists would interview the old people about Indigenous fire knowledge. The old people wouldn't tell them much. Understandably, they didn't trust them with such information.

Most of the time the researchers would leave thinking that the Elders knew nothing about fire at all. One scientist I met came to the conclusion that Aboriginal fire knowledge in Australia was lost forever. The Elders wouldn't tell them otherwise, simply because researchers weren't trusted in those times, and still aren't now for some. If they supported the Aboriginal aspirations for applying the knowledge, then it would be a different story. I've always believed that the best way to protect traditional knowledge is for Aboriginal people to apply their knowledge and culture and keep it alive. If Aboriginal people don't practice their culture, then their knowledge and land becomes more vulnerable.

That is why the Elders want to share the knowledge practically with the young people – it is the right method to pass on knowledge in a way that is complete. Demonstrating the Indigenous application of knowledge through the many fire workshops didn't exclude non-Indigenous people from coming and learning too. They needed to be involved so that everyone moves together, understanding how we all support the cause. But there have been occasions where the generosity of sharing knowledge has been taken advantage of as well. It's the mentality that can't seem to help itself from wanting to own and control everything. For me, I think it's important to understand what effects colonisation has had on our entire society.

In the beginning, dispossession was cast upon Indigenous people, then they were made to be dependent on the conqueror, then oppressed to make them do things the dominators' way. The effects of colonisation are still present in many countries today, except now it's worked its way deep into the subconscious of modern society. It is no longer devaluing just Aboriginal people into suppression, but this disillusioned way of thinking now infects every one of us. Dispossession, dependency and oppression. This combination is being enforced both intentionally and unintentionally, through gestures of love and hate. It is entrenched in such a way that even actions intended for good can contribute to the problem. My experiences have led me to believe that it is not just Aboriginal people who need to decolonise, but non-Aboriginal people as well.

The way Western science communicates knowledge is to separate everything into different categories and names. Separating knowledge is done by breaking down the values to give them their own separate findings. For example, Aboriginal fire knowledge is applied to the landscape to maintain the health of animals and plants. Science takes this aspect of Aboriginal fire knowledge and creates a new category called 'burning for biodiversity'. As a result, people think burning for biodiversity is different to Aboriginal fire practices. Some ecologist would come to three or four of our workshops and learn about fire from Aboriginal people, then go off and create their own project called 'ecological fire' and sell it differently.

Another value of Aboriginal fire practices is ensuring the country avoids major wildfires. It is a key goal of burning to keep the land and waters clean, to ensure the natural resources are not destroyed by mega-fires. The Western agencies have a fire they call hazard reduction or prescribed burning. This is where the land is burnt purely to avoid wildfire destroying the life and property of people.

The only component of Aboriginal fire they can't categorise is the spirituality side of the knowledge. Aboriginal fire management is then seen rather as a traditional hunting practice or ceremony. When knowledge is separated into different categories it becomes watered down. It also ricochets into forming divided mindsets and creates a fragmented knowledge base. A confusion of the right information that encourages the wrong application and interpretation, in this case of fire.

I've often been warned about sharing knowledge with Western institutions by many concerned people. But what can we do besides educate and involve everyone on the basics, in good faith, in hope that they do the right thing? Of course, I have seen countless researchers attend the workshops, write everything down and then disappear. Some don't even say hello or goodbye – just turn up, write everything down, and then go. Some will say, 'We're here to help you. Give us your information and we'll publish it and apply for funding for you.'

It's kind of the same as changing the patent of Aboriginal plant properties. Dissecting original knowledge until it comes out the other end with a different application and name. Maybe you can call it theft or a breach of protocol against the intellectual property rights of the knowledge holders. But in the end the watered-down version will have difficulties playing out the knowledge process; it usually does not provide all of the information or benefits compared with the original application. It is one thing to write Indigenous knowledge down, but there is a whole other process involved in applying the action.

The original application of Aboriginal fire knowledge requires you to learn about the country. To activate the landscape in a way that opens the doors to many other practices and opportunities. To be on country all the time in order to do the work of healing unbalanced landscapes. You can't be that culturally flexible and intimate with the land through the current Western burning programs.

Indigenous knowledge systems continue to be suppressed under Western control, unable to fully demonstrate their values right across the board. The effects this has had upon Aboriginal cultural responsibilities and aspirations are obvious to see. It's quite a scary situation, not only for Aboriginal people, but for non-Indigenous people as well. I refer to it as the knowledge gap.

The knowledge gap started right from when the old people were separated from their country. From there the loss of knowledge began as Aboriginal practices were ceased and Elders began to pass away without handing down the information. An ancient knowledge system totally devalued, and the beginnings of disadvantage to our environment and communities. In the earlier years in Australia, many non-Indigenous people did listen to Aboriginal people. I have been told many stories by elderly non-Indigenous farmers on how they learnt to burn to a degree from Aboriginal people. Some old-timers have told me about the good friendships they had, always helping each other out along the way.

Some folk would let the tribes walk through their declared properties and burn whenever they thought it was right. There was a historical knowledge of fire where the settlers learnt best practice from Aboriginal people in some places. Then eventually science along with mixed political views stopped burning with improved conservation. They stopped everyone from applying burning practices and put a total fire ban across the landscape. The period of taking people out of the land, then clearing much of it, and then eventually suppressing fire across the country was a big mistake. This not only happened in Australia, but many other countries around the world that are suffering fire problems today.

Since the banning of fire management practices, more Indigenous Elders have passed and even the old white fellas that learnt from Aboriginal people have also died and taken what they know with them. Today I get a large number of forty-year-old, third-generation farmers not knowing how to look after their land. They tell me stories where they remember being a kid seeing their grandfather riding on horseback burning the grass. But they were so young that they never got the chance to learn from the old-timers. The knowledge gap continued to grow, leaving many farmers not knowing what to do with inherited land that is sickened or under fire threat. Not only that, but they also face the legislation and laws to prevent them from exercising the knowledge to restrengthen it.

But it doesn't stop there: the knowledge gap is still growing in many ways within our society. There are the fire programs based on schemes where helicopters and planes fly around dropping water bombs on the country. I have met a few Elders that are concerned about such burning programs replacing the fine art of Aboriginal fire management. Another twenty years and more Elders will pass and the knowledge gap will continue to grow. 'Traditional burning' may end up as flying around in helicopters dropping fireballs on their country. Then the headlines will read, 'Traditional knowledge meets Western science'. It is certainly not a case of incendiary versus ground burning. We can use helicopters and technology in some cases, but encouraging the proper application of fire should always be first priority to maximise the benefits.

We need to be wise about having government agencies controlling Indigenous knowledge programs. There are higher chances of missing important layers of knowledge that can revive a wealth of understanding, solutions and opportunities. In the beginning we had Elders who were walking libraries, people with a wealth of knowledge. Now the majority of our society know very little about the land and have a lack of practical knowledge to draw from.

I've seen times where young people struggle with the simple task of boiling a billy by a camp fire. I've seen educated bosses without a clue be in charge of managing our country and agencies. It seems like our society is getting less wise, rather than getting smarter. People are lazier than before, less fit than before, have less connection with our planet. It's like we're going backwards in a few ways as an intelligent race, rather than forward.

People are made to depend on technical gadgets that read the wind, humidity, and calculate how much fuel is on the landscape. Depending on technology to tell how and when to burn rather than reading the land itself. It is a continuous spiral of humanity getting further disconnected from the land and a concern told to me by people from all walks of life. One thing is for sure: we cannot afford to go backwards anymore or become less wise than what we have already become. We cannot afford to have our society numbed while so much damage is being done to our weeping planet.

Some science will undermine Aboriginal fire knowledge practices. It's been said that Aboriginal people never burned the landscape at all. They publish this in the academic world as professionals of the Australian landscape. When stuff like this is posted on social media, many people believe it. What does that say for all of that amazing knowledge of fire from so many Aboriginal clan groups around Australia? All that information, all those stories, all their current fire practices, said to be a total lie or myth.

Science can be a powerful tool because people believe in it. It is like a religion for some; they believe everything that science says and nothing else unless science proves it. It's also common for people to think that science is always done for good, when in reality no one knows who gets that information and what they use it for. There has certainly been some bad fire science that I have seen over the years that is still influencing devastating environmental problems.

I would actually say that I love science, and it's cool what good science can do in all categories that enhances our lives. I am also excited about what it may bring in the future, that will be good for people and the planet. It's an amazing intelligence that the technical cultures bring to the table of humanity. But high scientific intelligence of technology is not the only intelligence mankind needs to survive. What's the point of having all the inventions, cars and machinery if the land is destroyed? Indigenous people bring the intelligence of sustainability and interconnectedness. The knowledge of how to live practically and spiritually with the land for so long without destroying the planet. Now that is also a crucial intelligence that humanity needs for a healthy, prolonged life on the planet – otherwise we won't have one.

I hope that Aboriginal knowledge will one day be fully supported by Western science. Where Indigenous knowledge in its respective fields gets the chance to become the science. A method where young knowledge respects old knowledge, the way that we teach our children. A good science, a practical science, a knowledge that originally comes from this land, its people and the spiritual dimensions from beyond. The Aboriginal science of Australia.

Part four

Sharing the fire knowledge

Chapter 14
The Traditional Knowledge Recording Project

When it came to exercising the passion for reviving Aboriginal knowledge, determination and heart were my main drive. There was so much energy put into getting things happening for our land and the people. Being in my late twenties, things were starting to move quite fast around recording the knowledge with video cameras. The earlier work of the Traditional Knowledge Recording Project created more interest, and many communities got on board. We started to help other Aboriginal communities through small recording workshops here and there. Some in other states started to show interest as well.

It wasn't long before some of them wanted a copy of the traditional knowledge database that was in the making, but it wasn't quite ready to be shared. Soon after, I was connected to UTS, the University of Technology in Sydney. They were happy to have me fly down to Sydney to show their technical experts where we were at with the database. The big city was new to me and was a real eye-opener compared to the small towns I was used to. I was pretty nervous to meet the university people and see what they might think of the work.

I had made one hundred and twenty different layouts, all mapped out into traditional knowledge categories. Performance and design-wise it was a totally clunky system, but at least it was clear on its intentions. After meeting with the technical experts, I soon learnt that they were amazed with the concept and design. They gave advice on how to move forward to strengthen the database so other communities could start using it.

I had no idea where to go from there, but it was at this time that I met a lady named Jacqueline from the university. Jacqueline Gothe was the senior lecturer of visual communication and design. She was a generation older than me and was drawn to the work with great interest. Little did I know that she would become a big part of my life and work. She shared the love I had for country, culture and the many Elders and communities involved. To cut a long story short, she soon became like family to me. She started to help wherever she could and in any way possible. She would do most of this under the radar, and we would always do things off the smell of an oily rag. Jacqueline lived with her artistic husband Michael Snape in Balmain, and they would put me up for the night when I was in town.

Because of the ongoing Traditional Knowledge Recording Project, Sydney started to become a regular place for me. It seemed to draw me there often to work with all sorts of talented people. They all became part of the journey and Jacqueline loved bringing them all together to create amazing outcomes. They helped technically and some helped with film projects out on country. It was a family-friendly space and everyone worked really well together, with heart.

Jacqueline eventually found a talented lady to help me with improving the database. With another stage of commitment and hard work, we managed to develop a robust version to share with other communities. The Elders were the pioneers of the initiative and, as a result, became more respected abroad. They were getting their pictures in newspaper articles and doing talks on radio stations. It made me feel proud, and watching them deal with the media was lots of fun. They deserved the attention and it was good to see them be acknowledged for such great work.

The idea of the Traditional Knowledge Recording Project and database was to give people the tools and process of reviving their own cultural knowledge. That meant understanding the many categories that make up the entire Indigenous knowledge system, and documenting how it was applied; conducting the entire practical process of cultural knowledge from start to finish; demonstrating the lores of land management with water, fire, plants, animals and significant places; and always making sure that we prepared and completed the whole process of each activity, in story and practice. Poppy taught me that nothing could be learnt unless it was lived, and so we relived the knowledge as much as possible to learn.

Finding ways to express this to people in theory became relevant, so that they could understand the process. I started drawing diagrams to try and communicate the knowledge revival process, and make it a little clearer. I found that there were three vital components to the completion of applying a knowledge practice. That is how the knowledge triangle came about, which isn't rocket science. A simple diagram to visualise the complete process of the practical knowledge transfer.

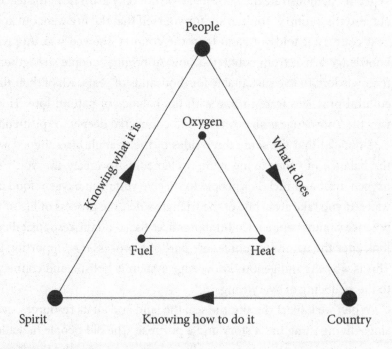

Side one of the triangle is knowing what it is.

Side two of the triangle is knowing what it does.

The final side that completes the triangle is knowing how to do it.

The knowing how to do it is the practical side of demonstrating knowledge. If that is missing, then the traditional transfer of passing on knowledge is not done accurately. The problem with society today is people are stuck on the knowing how to do it side of the triangle. For example, people know that wildfire is an environmental problem, they know that Indigenous fire knowledge is a solution, but they don't know how to do it. There are so many other situations where this same problem occurs from the breakdown of the practical knowledge transfer. When the practical side does not happen, the knowledge breakdown occurs until the practice of doing is lost.

The completion of the triangle represents practically applying traditional knowledge to create the benefits to you and the country. When we demonstrate the knowledge we not only learn from the teacher, but also the country. You can see for yourself that the fire went out at the next country: I told you, and then the country showed you. Applying knowledge learnt from country is how Aboriginal people strengthened their wisdom to live sustainably for thousands of years. All of their daily cultural practices were in line with the balance of natural lore. This is why the knowledge is so powerful and connected deeply to spirituality.

I noticed that the same three sides of the triangle also aligned with the balance of other living natural elements. To create fire you need oxygen, heat and fuel. For people to survive you need oxygen, food and water. If you take away one of the triangle sides, the process of life or the practice cannot happen. Cultural practices based on the responsibility to look after the natural resources are part of a process for supporting life. This is why the Indigenous knowledge system is holistic and connected to the wellbeing of everything.

When we look at the sky, the sea, the land and all its resources, every single living thing has a story and a purpose. The old people had a lore where every living thing was equally as important as each other. Over a few camp fire sittings, I drew diagrams that mapped these categories of knowledge in the sand. I put categories into their own circles and then drew lines connecting them to other knowledge fields they were related to. In the end I found myself drawing something that looked like some kind of knowledge map. To me, it was sort of like looking at the structure of humanity and our relationships with the planet and the universe.

I could see millions of invisible lines going back and forth constantly, connecting categories to each other like one big engine of life. How a bird was connected to a tree, and how that tree was connected to an animal, and how that animal connected that tree to the water, and how that water was connected to people; how the people's practice was connected to fire, and how the fire was connected to reviving country. It goes on and on and never stops. Like songlines going round and round all over the land and sea. Everything is connected to everything, dependent on each other in more ways than you could ever imagine. The Aboriginal knowledge system was so aligned with natural lore that the people become part of the living landscape.

When I looked at the knowledge map in relation to a cultural practice such as fire, I found that it benefited all of the categories. If the right ecosystem was burnt, the trees and the animals were protected, more fresh food plants grew and the health of that country improved. The same went for most other traditional practices. There were certainly no cultural practices that destroyed the water quality, and most of the plant and animal harvest was seasonal by lore. It wasn't surprising to find that all of the cultural practices respected everything else on the knowledge map.

When I took an example of some modern Western-based practices and compared them in the same way, many showed they did not benefit any of the categories. In fact, the only thing that benefited was what certain people got out of the action. Every other category on the knowledge map did not benefit and showed indicators of threat instead. It's not hard to work out that many modern practices involving the land and waters are not sustainable practices. Comparing human activity to the knowledge map was a clear way to see if the practice was in line with natural lore.

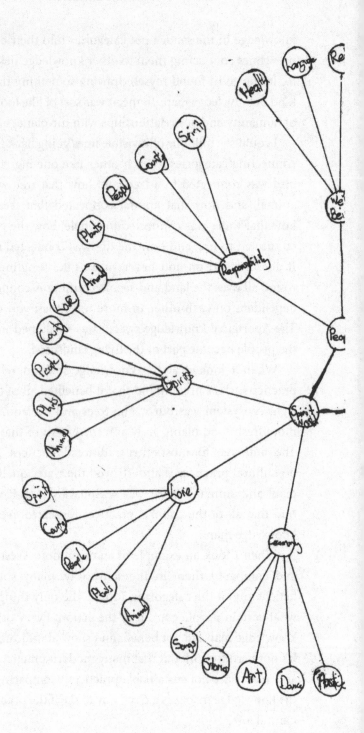

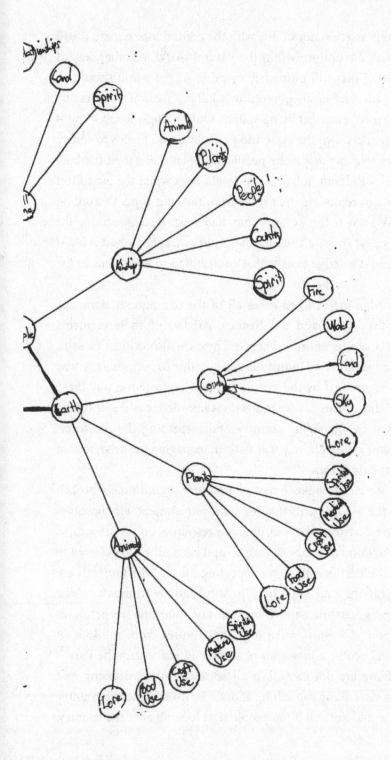

If a human practice is not in line with the natural lore system, it will eventually cause disruption within the natural world. Another way of saying it is a well that will ultimately run dry. As the world should be aware by now, such actions begin to slowly kill our natural resources by disrupting the interrelational living system. Once a single living thing is destroyed, it breaks down the cycle and everything else begins to suffer.

Poppy once told me that if the people of the land die, then the land will slowly die with them. It had started right back when the First Fleet arrived and began removing the people from the landscape. Disrupting an integrated knowledge system that had sustained Australia for thousands of years. They had no idea that Aboriginal people had evolved a sophisticated knowledge system that contributed to a sustainable life on Earth.

The knowledge map incorporates all of the five natural elements: earth, wind, fire, water and the cosmos. All five of these elements are the masters of our entire existence. They are also critical tools in allowing the application of Indigenous knowledge to happen. The way the elements are treated by the people can also regulate the way these super forces behave. This is why Indigenous knowledge and spirituality is highly based on managing country and respecting the life force. Managing country the right way will assist in managing the behaviour of the elements the right way.

Today we see clear evidence that natural lore is continually broken and it is then the five elements that serve the punishment. Fire becomes destructive and destroys all of our precious resources on the landscape. Water begins to flood or die by drying up and becoming too polluted to support life. The Earth's soils stop supporting life and the minerals are not there to clean the land and water. The wind and the cosmos combine rage and deliver greater damage from storms or abnormal temperatures like we see now. The sun's warming temperatures from millions of miles away can become a diagnosis of chronic illness within the Earth's atmosphere if we are not careful. It all seems a little depressing, but maybe we can start doing something about it by listening to the country again. Poppy would say that if the people start looking after the country, everything can come good again.

No matter what we do, the system of natural lore will always be relevant today. Even modern technology can assist in the process of activating traditional knowledge values. Having knowledge recorded with technology is a good thing, but having the knowledge living within the people will always be far better. Knowledge was passed down and stories kept for thousands of years without the use of modern technology.

But technology is now a part of these times, though as a personal precaution, I try to keep technology as a tool rather than overtaking my life completely. It is crucial that future generations are influenced by practical human application rather than only by technology itself. A dear elderly lady friend of mine once commented to me about this subject, saying, 'You can shoot for the stars, but never forget where you come from.' Meaning that we could use the modern tools and technology, but keep everything connected to the principals of lore, culture and country. We also do not know what effect technology may have on our children in the future. We need to remember that technology has been a major player in taking the younger generations away from culture and the country as well.

The Traditional Knowledge Recording Project got a lot of interest and the concept got the attention of other cultures and countries. It was the first time that I had the chance to present the work overseas, which was exciting. As a result, I soon realised that other Indigenous communities had similar stories to our own. I found that the knowledge map structure was also a similar fit for other Indigenous cultures from around the world. It was a really exciting experience to meet many other communities and share the work with them. The first interest was from communities in North America, and then New Zealand.

It was these cultural exchanges that gave me the opportunity for one very memorable trip I'll never forget. It was the time I was asked to present the program to the Sámi people of northern Finland and met a passionate traditional knowledge revivalist named Tero Mustonen. Tero is a Finnish person dedicated to revitalising the traditions of his people. He is also the leader of his village, named Selkie, in the North Karelia part of the country and he works for the Snowchange Cooperative. Snowchange Cooperative supports a network of local and Indigenous cultures around the world, particularly within the northern regions. Through Snowchange, Tero is a great advocate for tackling climate change in his region and bringing this awareness to the world's attention.

The Finns and the Sámi share a linguistic connection. Snowchange had been working with the Sámi for over ten years and Tero was keen to take me way up to the north of the country to help some of the communities there with the knowledge recording concept. To make matters even more interesting, he invited me to go in the middle of winter. It was the first time I was travelling around in minus-twenty-degree temperatures. We started our long two-day drive north, covering hundreds of kilometres. There was no sunlight at all, just a dark, freezing landscape outlining trees covered in ice and snow. I was rugged up all the time, with a fox skin hat Tero gave me and layers upon layers of warm clothing.

We also had a Sámi Traditional Owner and former president of the Sámi Council, Pauliina Feodoroff, with us as a part of the mission. She was looking forward to managing her own recording project for her Skolt Sámi group and country. It was so cool to meet these traditional people whose skin colour was as fair as the snow covering their landscape, and to see that they had the same values for culture and country as our people back home.

But nothing could have prepared me for what I was about to experience next. As we drove along the icy road, Tero offered to take me to one of their rock-art sites along the way. My ears pricked up at the words 'art site' and I was curious about what he had in store. We finally pulled over to the side of the road and then I followed him along a rough bush track littered with wild blueberry bushes and pine trees that paved the way to the ancient paintings.

When we entered the art site I was totally amazed to see Saraakallio, a rocky cliff wall sitting on the edge of a big, beautiful icy lake. I walked in, noticing that the parent rock was actually granite (just like some art sites in Australia). When I looked at the pigment it appeared to be just like our ochre, and similar shades of red and yellow. The paintings were two-dimensional like ours too, with similar gestures being displayed by the human images. I looked at a painting of an animal and it was a similar style to those at home, except this one was a moose and ours was a kangaroo.

Everything I was seeing seemed to show that people were once connected to the land and other living creatures here, the same as Indigenous people in Australia. Tero then went on to guide me down toward the edge of the deep, freezing waters of the lake. He stood there gazing into the water and began to tell me a story. 'Many of the artefacts and tools that belonged to the clans who created these paintings are at the bottom of this lake. Christian priests forbade the uses of our sacred places when they arrived.' He went on to tell me that traditional people of the area worshipped the trees – they were the tree people. The Catholic and later the Lutheran priests gave orders to chop down all of the sacred trees. Many of their sacred places were destroyed by these colonisers and replaced with a church. It all started happening right back in the twelfth century, he explained.

I stood there thinking deeply about how Indigenous people worldwide had endured the arrival of 'the coming of the light'. It seemed to be the beginning of erasing culture and taking people away from the country. They wanted the people to worship the priests and the church and not the earth. Replacing spirituality with religion, exchanging the bible for the land. Whether the people bowed down to this power or not, they were ultimately subjected to genocide and their lands taken from them. Are all the white people's ancestors Indigenous and they don't know it? Questions started floating around in my head and it was quite disturbing, really.

Tero said it was time to go and he looked a little spooked by something. He felt that an ancestral spirit was starting to create a presence and that we should leave the site immediately. My hair started to stand as we left and I felt a strong surge of a greater understanding run rapidly through my veins like cold water. Yep, everything culturally, spiritually and historically was just like home, no different to how our mob connect culturally and spiritually.

We continued our journey, driving on the freezing, snowy roads. Being in this part of the world had another special curiosity that was personal to me. My ancestors from my father's side came from this area of the globe as well. It wasn't exactly Finland, but the Steffensen name I bear came from the Scandinavian regions of Denmark, Norway and Sweden. People I met along the way would tell me that my name traditionally came from those areas.

I learnt that Sweden and Norway was once traditional Sámi country, before it was taken from them. I was a product of Indigenous people and boat people as well. Like many people today, a mixed bag of lollies with a few bloodlines, but true and proud to be who I am. Either way, it was fascinating to learn more about my ancestral self and connections. In the end I was lucky enough for Tero to drive me into Norway, to the shores of the Arctic Ocean. He stood me on the stony coastline and told me that my ancestors once sailed these icy oceans long ago. I stood there in deep thought, looking over the cruel, dark sea with shores of barren, jagged rocks. It made me feel privileged to be standing there while imagining the passing sailing ships in those days. I stood there, thinking of my colourful history – that I had the blood and the love for the land and the sea. I stared into that ocean, realising that reconnecting with culture and country was important for people all over the world.

We continued our journey and Tero took me to a house of an Elder, master fisherman Olli Klemola in Pälkäne, where there was a small gathering of the Snowchange people. They warmly took me in and fed me their traditional foods as we talked of our visit. There were a few men and women of all ages and they were all cultural people. The time came where I was invited to go off with the men to a traditional sauna, to talk among ourselves. It was the same lore like at home, where men's business and women's business are still conducted. I followed the group out of the house and into the cold night for a short walk through the snow to another old building. It was a large, two-hundred-year-old sauna that could fit quite a few people at one time. As I walked into the building I was instantly struck by its old appearance and ancient craftsmanship. There was no electricity in most of the villages I visited and the saunas were heated with wood-fuelled fires. This one had a massive steel cauldron on the lower level of the building and then the sauna area on the top level. It was a special place to have gatherings and talks, because it was so important to their culture.

We all prepared to enter the sauna and before long I found myself sitting with the group in the steaming, dark room in a meeting-like manner. Olli, the old man, started to talk about his people and country, and how important it was to keep their culture alive. We shared thoughts on ways forward and it soon became a very powerful conversation. The old man started to talk about his frustrations about all the things going wrong with his people and land. He started to curse the early invaders of his lands and referred to how these influences came from mainland Europe to Finland. 'Those Europeans (Indo-Europeans) initiated the damages affecting our waters and taking away our traditional culture. Later, the Finns did much of the damage to themselves when they forgot their traditions.'

I closed my eyes as I listened to that old man and it was no different to hearing the old people talking back home. The Indigenous people here had the same problems happening to their communities and country as we do. 'It is terrible what early Europeans did and then subsequently what our own people have done to our country,' Olli went on, leading the conversation with his long hair and beard now drenched in sweat from the steam rising from the cauldron below.

Being that I was with the white, traditional and Indigenous Sámi peoples of the world, I couldn't help but ask them a question that was lingering in my mind.

'Are you sure that calling the invaders Europeans is the right term?'

Everyone went into a small space of silence for a moment and started nodding their heads slowly. I could just see the old man's face, lit up by the fire heating the giant cauldron. He turned towards the group and started to muffle some alternatives. We soon came to the agreement to call the ones with no respect for culture and Mother Earth the disconnected people. 'Those disconnected people, that's right, they are the disconnected ones', the old man happily admitted aloud.

Questions started running through my mind once again. Where did these disconnected people come from? How do we connect them back with the planet and culture again?

Being separated from the land has been entrenched for so long that the disconnected people are now everywhere, in every shape and form. There are even Aboriginal people that have become disconnected too. Today the disconnected people come in all colours, from black, white, brindle and brown. There was a deeper understanding that I was starting to become aware of and it seemed to be a connection that underpins us all.

Once again, this is why the revival of the traditional knowledge work was so well received. But in the end I came to the conclusion that archiving the knowledge in a database was not the answer. For one, it is totally boring sitting in front of a computer archiving stuff, and two, information sitting on a shelf does nothing good for nobody. Archiving is a Western management system, based on documenting data and putting it on a shelf to collect dust. If we were going to revive traditional knowledge, then it needed to be done by putting it back into the people, and not a computer.

Once I came to that conclusion I dropped the database and never picked it up again. It was so obvious that the old people were trying to install the knowledge into me and not the camera. We hadn't recorded hardly anything at all compared to what was stored within my head. The database did phase away slowly, though some communities still wanted to record knowledge, and that was fine. After all, it is so important to record the old people before we lose them. But I wanted to focus on strengthening the practical traditional knowledge transfer. To get the young people out on country learning firsthand within their own environment. To build on their own knowledge and activate their own culture, so it is revived and living. Fire was a good way to start that process.

Chapter 15

Go ahead

Meanwhile back on Awu-Laya country, the national parks rangers seemed to leave us alone for a little while. This allowed us to get back to the joys of exercising cultural practices on country in peace. As usual, Poppy and old man TG would be waiting for me with fishing lines, swags and a billy tin. Things were going good and we could concentrate on being free with the country. We were attracting a little attention around our fire management efforts; we started to get noticed by a range of other agencies who were interested in what we were doing.

Not long after, I got a call from an Aboriginal community from New South Wales asking for help with their own fire projects. They asked if I could go down to work with them on their country. I wasn't sure at the time; it seemed a bit risky to go to someone else's country and teach them Indigenous burning. I turned down the offer and stayed focused with our own work, but I did have an interest in seeing the country down south. I wanted to see more country and broaden my knowledge on reading other landscapes.

Over the years we would hear about the many massive wildfires that were going on in the southern parts of Australia. I remember a few occasions of sitting with the Elders, watching the reports on the news. The old people would sit there feeling really sorry for the people and the country. They would constantly say that the people are not looking after the country. 'They need to believe us, do like we do,' Poppy would say. 'We need to go there and show them how to do.' The old people were really serious when they said these things. They hated seeing the destruction of the country, and more so when lives and houses were taken by these wild infernos.

Every time a bad fire would make the news the topic would always be mentioned among many Elders in our region. I remember when a special old woman I respected commented on the situation one time during a film interview. 'I don't know why the country, the houses and the people get burnt, when there are so many people right there to look after the land.' It made her really angry, even though it wasn't her country. The passion she expressed that day even for someone else's country was strong through and through. So strong that the old lady shed a tear for Mother Earth. 'We made this into a rich country with everything here, and now they have come to destroy it. It's not a lucky country anymore. When we go, it will be finished, no more lucky country.' She said all this so powerfully that I started wiping tears away from my eyes as I looked through the camera lens.

We have large wildfires in the far northern parts of Australia too. The old people were constantly upset when they saw local bushland burnt to a cinder by wildfire during the hotter seasons. The only difference between the wildfires up north and the ones down south is the loss of life and property. If we had loss of life and property with our wildfires up north, it would've been on the news too. The loss of the land, trees, plants and animals from fire is so great, and there was hardly any mention of that or how Aboriginal knowledge could help back then. That is what made the old people sad the most, the fact that no one listened to the Aboriginal people of this country.

Poppy had visited the southern parts of Australia earlier in his life, through his police tracking days. He talked about how he could read the country down south the same way as reading his own. The police used to get him to find lost people all over the place. He was among the best of police trackers in his day, and it was always amazing to watch him in action. You have to know how to read country to become a good tracker. That old man could track on any terrain and he was always proud to tell the stories of the adventures he had. He found a few lost people in the bush over his time, and became respected. The tales he told of reading country a couple of thousand kilometres away from his own land really stuck in my mind.

For some reason, the thought of helping communities in other parts of the country was also in my mind, and then the call to go down south came around again. Again, the old fellas didn't want to travel so I asked if I could give it a go for the first time. Poppy and old man TG gave their blessings, and wanted me to go and help them. I didn't know who I was meeting up with, but I was excited that I was going to see the southern country. I wanted to see different country and experience what Poppy was talking about with reading the indicators. With a little organising, I soon found myself travelling to New South Wales, close to the Victorian border. I was greeted by the Traditional Owners and they showed me around a couple of locations on their country.

The first site they took me to was a large gum-tree forest. My first impressions were that it didn't look too healthy. The poor country had suffered a very hot wildfire almost twenty years ago. As I walked into the country, I noticed that it was the same as our gum-tree country, but different. Even the soil was the same colour to home – but I was shocked to see that the gum-tree country I was standing in didn't have any grass, herbs or small plants around it at all. It only had a very thin layer of leaves on the ground and that was about it. There were some little native shoots among mainly weeds here and there, but otherwise not much at all.

I slowly walked through the country with the sound of crunching leaves beneath my feet, looking around for what I could see on the forest floor. There was no sign of life, not a single sound of any small creature scurrying through the dead leaves. There were no birds singing and the tree canopies were stunted, bearing more dead branches than live ones. I had never seen gum-tree country so unhealthy, and it was quite sad. The country had been burnt so badly in the past that it still hadn't recovered. Even after twenty years, it was still showing no signs of getting back to health.

I told the people my observations and it seemed to make sense to them. They agreed, because they were looking for certain plant species that they knew culturally about but couldn't find anywhere. They took me to other areas which did not look much better than the first. I was taking everything in as I tried to get acquainted with the country through the guidance of the custodians. They went on to tell me that it would be almost impossible to get the fire and environment authorities to allow them to burn. But it was a small start in moving forward, and it was a good day for everyone all the same. In the end I wished them well and started on my journey back home. My mind was ticking overtime on what I had just experienced.

When I got back home, the first thing I told the old people was that the gum-tree country had no grass at all, just leaves on the ground. They couldn't believe what they were hearing. 'Can't be!' they yelled out. 'That's really no good.' I went on to tell them about seeing and hearing no animals, and how the trees were stunted and burnt. Poppy responded simply by saying that they don't know how to burn. He went on to say that the old people would fix that country if they saw it like that. 'Them old people from before, if they see the country like that, they wouldn't just leave it, they will fix 'em up again. Burn them a little bit and burn 'em again, till he come right then.' I understood completely what the old fellas were talking about, and things were starting to click together.

After that I started to think a lot more about being able to fix sick country like the one I had seen. After seeing that country, I was confident that the right fires could heal that kind of land. I was hoping that one day the opportunity might just come along. In the meantime I was back into burning Awu-Laya country with the old fellas and families again. Time always went by fast when we were out on country, living with the seasons. There was always plenty to do and the more we went on country the more work they wanted to do.

Pete was still there on occasion, asking questions about things for the PhD, which always led to creating more burns and assessments to document the information. More burns in different systems were needed for the study and, like always, I went to discuss the request with Poppy. I had been asking him for permission to do things for over twelve years now and this time something different happened. He gave me the permission to go and burn country on my own for the first time without him.

I stood there in surprise, not knowing what to say. In my mind I was uncomfortable doing anything without the old people. But Poppy continued on, telling me to go ahead and that he was staying home this time to rest. But old man TG was always still there to fill the front seat of the Toyota. There was no way he was gonna let me leave him behind. Poppy still came along on trips; it just meant that he would also let me burn country on my own.

A few days later I was out on country again, this time with just Poppy, his grandsons Dale and Lewis, and a couple of other young men. Poppy insisted that we take the camera because he wanted to record some stories. So we suited up and were out there recording trees and country once again. Today we had the young lads watching, so that always made the old man perform at his best. I pressed the record button on the camera and gave the old man the hand sign to start yarning. But this time he didn't start telling stories about the land or culture. He started delivering a message about wanting the kids to take over looking after the country.

He went on for a quite a while, going through all of the families' names and stating roles they had to play and country to look after. Basically, he was stating his own requests on camera and that was all he wanted to talk about that day. It was a real honour to listen to him and I knew that he was delivering an important message. I had never seen him talk to the camera like he did on that day and it made my hair stand up a little.

The late afternoon arrived and Poppy and I were burning near Rocky Creek, which was a creek that ran through his country. The young men were all gone, scoping the river for barramundi. It was another magic moment where we were at peace with the land, watching the burns trickling away as the sun slowly set. Poppy pointed out some mixed tea-tree and box country, and commented on how nice the native grasses were coming back. 'One day when you come back, you will see the country nice and green. You can leave it then, boy, don't have to burn it.'

We were burning that patch of country all the time because it was a bit sick with weeds and too much tea-tree. He was saying that you could keep it from burning for a year or two once the country is healthy again. 'How will I know that?' I asked. He told me that I would know when I see it. 'When I am gone, the country will keep teaching you.' It was a powerful moment, and then there was silence. I watched the old man gazing over his land and it was like he was seeing it in the times when his people were free. As I watched alongside him, at that moment I knew that this work must never stop, it needs to carry on.

After that day I headed back to Cairns to do some work on editing film and be with my two children. There were still other communities that needed help with recording knowledge, and I was helping them. By now it was early February in the year 2006. That night I was woken by the phone in the early hours of the morning. It was those few words I didn't want to hear: 'We lost the old man.'

Devastated by the news, I broke down for a while to take in what I just heard. I thought of our last moments together and through my sadness I thought fondly of his cleverness. He was a great man and I have never met anyone who knew fire the way he did, to this day. Poppy had died on 9 February 2006 and many people mourned the loss of a true legend of the Cape. An Awu-Laya man, Mey Romi.

Chapter 16
Fire and the Story

After losing the old man, the community wasn't the same. As expected, it took a while for the families to recover. Old man TG was devastated; he had lost his big brother and lifelong partner in surviving those hard days together. It took at least three years before the old man could feel comfortable in heading out onto country again. Everything we did on the land reminded him of his brother, and he would break down every time. It was really hard to see him like this, and everyone respected that and gave him time to heal.

We didn't go out to Saxby for the first year or two because of sorry business. Saxby was the old man's place, so we couldn't go there until the sorry business was over. Instead, I ended up taking TG on trips with me to help other communities who were still doing the Traditional Knowledge Recording. We had a bit going on with that program in the Cape to keep the old man busy. This also led us to working on fire with the other communities as well. He was always keen to travel to nearby communities, and everyone loved him visiting their country. He would encourage the other communities to record their knowledge and look after their land with fire too. Everywhere we went, he would score another badge from the local community ranger services to sew onto his shirt. Keeping busy wasn't hard to do for that old man.

As time started to heal a little more, old TG's spirit was showing signs of getting a little stronger. We wanted to focus on fire again and pick up from where his brother had left off. The idea came up to create our own documentary about fire to honour the old people and all the work we had done. I sketched down some plans and then we came up with making a film called *Fire and the Story*. It ended up being our own little classic and it happened magically with very little organising. We didn't have any budget at all, but managed to create a one-hour documentary on the back of field trips. I added some old footage of Poppy and TG, and then combined it with some fresh shoots to put the story together.

This time we involved other Elders from the region who shared the passion to get involved, from Aurukun, Yalanji country, and Kuranda. I even managed to create a scene that involved a Miwok (Native American) by the name of Don Hankins, living near Chico, California. I had shot the film with him when I had the opportunity of visiting that country for the Traditional Knowledge Recording Project delegation trip. Meeting Don was an interesting experience because it was the first time that I got to talk about fire with another Indigenous person from the other side of the world.

Don gave me the opportunity to meet some of the people there and see a bit of the country. He took me to one location where the forest floor was pretty much the same as the gum country that I saw in New South Wales. The ground had no grass and it was covered in just leaves, and he complained of the absence of native plants and grasses. I looked at the soils and saw that it was a rich, dark soil, which meant that it should be lush and green with vegetation. I considered the similarities to our country at home, and shared my thoughts with him on timing to recover the land with fire. I then filmed him talking about the place, not knowing where the footage may go at the time.

Later on, Don ended up putting the match to that site and the results were just as we expected. He sent me photographs of green grasses and butterflies in place of what was just dead leaves. Some of the vegetation was not native, but it was a great start all the same. He was pretty happy with the outcome, but that was probably the only place the authorities would let him burn at the time. Not only did we have similarities with our cultural practices, but also with governments restricting Indigenous rights. It was way harder for him to get a fire happening on his country, and I don't think he could be as forceful as we were in getting our first fires happening. He did secretly show me how to burn a tiny area in the pine forests, which was amazing to see. The flame was so low as it cleaned the forest floor to make way for his traditional foods.

There were so many similarities in what fire meant for the Native Americans compared to our own fire practices in Australia. The deer was just like our kangaroo, it was attracted to fire too. They came to eat the fresh grass shoots, lick the ash and sometimes bathe in it to clean themselves from parasites. I got the chance to go on a bus ride with a group of Elders from other areas to look at their country. Once again, listening to them talking about the landscape was no different to home. 'Oh, there are no berries growing in the forest anymore. There used to be berries everywhere when we were children.' Their land was choked up with dead vegetation and weeds because their fire practices had stopped the same way as our own had in Australia. I came to realise there must be so many places and cultures on the planet suffering from the same syndrome of sick country.

Overall, it was good to add that bit of footage I took with Don into our fire documentary. It was a bonus to add content from overseas to a film that didn't have any budget. But I was becoming pretty good at making things happen with no money, making everything happen along the way. The spirits were helping too, because everything would eventually fall into place most of the time. In the end we finished the film, which seemed to do pretty well in getting the message across for those who saw it. We never really had much support to get the film out there except for some DVDs that we managed to put together.

A good friend of mine by the name of Claire Brunner, from a charitable fund called Donkey Wheel, helped us out to show the film in Sydney and Melbourne. We hired a venue in each city and took down a number of the people involved to help make it happen. We even sang songs and had traditional dance before we showed the film. But I don't think people were ready to hear about Indigenous fire knowledge at that time. I never had much experience in advertising a gig in a major city either. The Sydney show went pretty well, but in Melbourne we ended up giving out free tickets on the street just to get people to come. Some of the dancers got painted up and went out onto the street to hand out tickets. Even then we couldn't give them away.

As I was trying to hand out tickets to the massive passing crowds some people yelled out, 'It's all bullshit.' There was a little too much disrespect in the air and it started to make my heart feel sick. 'Don't you want to learn how to protect yourself and the country from wildfires?' I yelled back. More horrible comments were thrown in return and I gave up in the end. I understood that people were busy carrying on with their city lives, but most didn't give a damn on that day. I think we were a little ahead of our time, despite the fact that bushfires were already destroying life and property in the region. It wasn't the response that I had been hoping for, but at least we tried. A couple of years later, I was watching the news reporting the 2009 wildfires burning thousands of hectares and destroying life and property throughout Victoria. I sat and watched, then turned off the television because I couldn't watch no more.

But when we did get back from Melbourne that time, we were proud of our film. It was well received by all the families and communities at home. Everyone that saw the film gave good reviews, so that made it all worthwhile. Eventually it got a run on the local Indigenous television station. People would always tell me that they saw it, and it started to get the message out there. I started receiving calls from communities in many parts of Australia interested in getting the good fire into their own country. I had no idea how that might happen, but it made me realise there were lots of communities out there needing help. After the television station finished running the film, it was never showed on air again.

Chapter 17

The Indigenous Fire Workshop

With all the changes happening as time went by, the PhD Pete was doing slowed down for me and old TG. But Pete had done enough work with us on country to keep plodding along with the task. It had been going for about three years now, and I think she would have many more years to go before it was finished. She ended up getting a job with a local natural resource management organisation. That kept her busy with lots of land management projects with many communities around the Cape. It was a good thing because at least she could still work on fire with communities on occasion.

It was in these times that we got the chance to start doing Indigenous fire workshops with the local communities. The idea of the workshop was to educate and strengthen Indigenous fire knowledge with other clan groups in the area. Old man TG was keen to get Aboriginal rangers out on country to learn the fire knowledge. It was the first time that we were involving other communities in such a way. The location for our first workshop was in Lama Lama country in Rinyirru (Lakefield) National Park, at a place called Bizant. It was only a small workshop of about thirty people and we all knew each other well.

We all walked the land together, burning country and talking about the different trees and country types. It was lots of fun and all of the participants got right into it as they learnt firsthand on country. It was a moment of empowerment and I could see straight away that the workshop was a good idea. Everybody took turns at being interviewed on camera, expressing their feelings about the day. Old TG was the happiest of all as he sat in the long grass watching from under a shady tree, smoking his pipe. He made sure that everyone got a turn to talk to the camera about what they were learning. Nothing made him more happy than to see his people back on the land looking after it again.

After the success of the first workshop, things started to move towards running another one. People began to hear about the workshop and it eventually generated interest from clan groups in southern Australia. I discussed the idea of inviting them up north with old TG, and he was more than happy to have them come along. The old man liked the idea of having visitors from down south coming up to learn on his country. Pete managed to obtain partnerships and support through her job, and that got the ball rolling. We ended up having about seventy people registered at the next workshop and half of them were from New South Wales communities. Many of them were coming up north for the first time and they were pretty excited about camping in crocodile country.

The southerners experienced something special that most of us up north take for granted every day: the freedom to burn country without any fire trucks or authorities telling us what to do. They commented on how easy it was for us to burn because we didn't have life and property all around us. There were miles of red tape for them to go through just to even think about the idea. It was such a pleasure to give them the experience of fire with so much freedom and Aboriginal leadership. Walking through the country with the fire, pointing out all of the indicators of knowledge along the way. Most of them had never been that close to a fire and some were even more stoked to personally light the grass themselves. For many of them it was one of the best days of their lives, and you could feel a strong vibe of excitement and happiness in the air.

It made me realise how much this valuable knowledge had been missing for many Indigenous people. It was clear to see that these fire workshops needed to keep on going, bringing everyone together to learn from each other. The supporting agencies continued to help find some funds to help bring the next workshop to reality. There was never any certainty that funding would be available and it became harder to find the support. This led us to charging a fee for people to attend, which people had no problem in accepting. It was the only way it was going to survive, by the people keeping it alive. One year we ran the workshop with hardly any funds at all and I found myself paying some of the bills from my own money. It ran at a loss here and there, but it was always an amazing workshop regardless.

Everyone who attended chipped in and helped out when things got a little harder to handle. We had to build our kitchens from scratch at times and hunt fresh meat from the bush just to feed people. We would have a small hunting party fishing for barramundi, and then shoot our own clean-skin cow to feed the hungry campers. We set up donkey systems for hot water and dug holes in the ground for people to use as a toilet. The worst part was carting portable toilets over rough dirt roads for hours – it was certainly doing things the hard way because of the limited budget. But that was the early days of getting the workshops happening and we still had a lot of fun. People understood the situation and got involved, and that is the main reason it always did so well.

Each year more people would come to experience the workshop and then go back to their homelands to tell of their adventures. It started to get a lot of interest and within a few workshops we'd had almost two hundred people attend. Each year the workshop went to a different community of the Cape to demonstrate the diversity of ecosystems and land management problems. It also gave the local clan groups a chance to host the event and get their rangers involved in the delivery. Eventually the little Cape York Indigenous Fire Workshop started to attract mainstream people of all types. We started to get people from the Rural Fire Service, NSW national parks, government agencies, and pastoralists. Everyone wanted to come up north to learn about Indigenous fire management practices.

The workshop developed into breaking people into groups to do different practical presentations throughout the event. We had our local

Indigenous bioscientist Gerry Turpin lead the botanical workshops. We involved Pete, who helped with the monitoring techniques developed from the PhD. There were film workshops and interviews with all the participants in support of the initiative. Burning workshops and reading country, with the Traditional Owners of the area hosting and leading the way. The local clans would lead tours of their country which gave people the big picture of fire and culture.

There was always live music and entertainment in the evenings using the talents of our presenters and communities. Just about everyone involved had musical talents, which is not surprising in any Indigenous gathering. Every year the workshop got better and better, and it started to become something really special for everyone.

People came from all over the country, bringing people of different backgrounds, race, occupation and opinion. They would all come with their own perspectives, and by the end they would all leave on the same page. The participants started to develop a network and inspired each other to get fire projects happening on their own country. It was a great thing, but there was still a long way to go in dealing with the challenges. Having the workshop open for all people to attend also meant dealing with all kinds of attitudes.

One year we held a workshop back on Awu-Laya country, to keep things going for old TG and the families. It was a great time for the old man's grandsons, Lewis and Dale, to step up and start talking for their country, since the loss of their grandfather. The young men led the burning workshop and had groups of people following them around country for three days. It was a proud moment for them and, as always, they burnt the country with no shoes on their feet. We burnt Awu-Laya country barefoot with the old people; it was the way we had always done it. We lit up the fine, fiery grass of the tea-tree country in front of our audience, then walked barefoot across the burnt ground straight afterwards, to present what was happening with the fire and country.

People were amazed that we could walk across the burnt ground following the fire with no shoes. Everyone was okay with the situation except a small group of fire officers from New South Wales. They were not impressed at all with the barefoot burning techniques. They started to make a fuss and it soon leaked out to the whole workshop group. They had come to old TG's country to learn so much beautiful knowledge through an Aboriginal burning experience, but instead all they could reflect on was their complaint that the presenters had no shoes on.

While doing the workshops I came across a few people like this, and it was those that I didn't enjoy sharing the knowledge with. Other non-Indigenous people like scientists, researchers and ecologists would also come along and write everything down and take it away. I started to get a little worried about what they might do with the knowledge without involving or acknowledging Aboriginal people. It was a situation where the workshops were so important for the community that it outweighed the gamble of information being misused by Western institutions.

Teaching the fire knowledge in a public workshop was always going to be dangerous in many ways, but we can't exclude the white fella. We needed them on board too if we are going to put Aboriginal fire knowledge into the mainstream. We need to educate non-Indigenous people on the traditional fire as well, but in a way where Aboriginal people lead the process. Making sure the workshop focused on empowering Indigenous communities to run their own fire programs was key to sharing knowledge the right way.

The fire workshop was a great place to start giving the communities an experience with fire and creating networks. But more importantly, the people need to learn on their own country. What they were learning at the Cape York workshops was only the tip of the iceberg. There were so many country types to learn about, and you couldn't learn them all in a couple of days. People were continuing to invite me down to their country to help them and I was gathering the courage and experience to take up the offer.

I went to discuss going down south to help communities once more with old man TG. 'Yeah, boy, you go', he said. I knew he wanted me to go, but still I had doubts about leading such an activity. 'What if the people don't like what I'm doing?' I asked him. What if I made a mistake, and what would people think of me teaching this knowledge? The old man slowly looked up at me and simply said, 'It don't matter who you are, boy, as long as you do the right thing.' As long as I stuck to the truth, stood by the right people for country I would be alright. His words gave me great strength as I sat there beside him, thinking about the uncharted journeys ahead.

Chapter 18
For country and spirit

It was the end of one of the earlier workshops and I had just got back to Cairns to unload the four-wheel drive. It was the afternoon and I ended up having to lie down for a while. I looked up at the ceiling, and slowly closed my eyes. As I drifted off I was startled by a strong voice whispering in my ear, 'Old TG is getting weak.' I opened my eyes in fright. I laid there with my eyes open, still hearing those words in my head.

I thought for a moment and realised that old TG was becoming more dependent on his walking stick. I took it as a sign that things were going to slow down a bit and that it was time for him to take it easy. He was becoming too weak to travel around with me on long, hard journeys. He even started to turn down trips out on country himself, which was a sure sign he was slowing down. His back was playing up and driving on the dirt roads wasn't good for him in the end. 'You go, boy, I'm going to stay here and rest.' It was sad to hear those words from him, after all the adventures and good times we'd had together. It was even sadder to look at the empty passenger seat as I drove my four-wheel drive to places from that day on.

Living in between Laura and Cairns and keeping connected to old man TG and my own family became harder to maintain. I had done everything possible to continue doing the work we had started, but it was all slowing down a little from no support. I tried getting funding through the corporate world, applying for grants with the government, or partnerships with land councils and corporations. None of those shoes fitted my feet and all of them were hard to deal with, as they were always political and there were too many other hidden agendas. I had to find a way to get on my own so I could work freely and directly with the communities and country.

My personal experience with the funding world was horrible, as it would always stress me out. There was plenty of time wasted on trying to write applications to find money and then producing reports at the end of it. You also need an authorised, trustworthy organisation to administrate the funds, which can also create problems. Waiting to get money before you could even go out and do any action. A lot of time was spent dealing with that reporting side of things rather than going out to do the actual work. Of course, it did teach me heaps along the way, but it felt like a system that was set up to fail. Either way, I didn't like the feel of it all and I wanted to get as far away from it as possible. Not to say that funding isn't good – it is crucial to make lots of great things happen for many people in the world. It just created too many headaches for me to do what I wanted to do at that time.

In the end I found myself learning how to create my own business and that opened up another world of understanding. I asked old TG if I could call the business an Awu-Laya name and he agreed to call it Mulong. Mulong means 'spirit' and it seemed like an appropriate name for what I was doing. But I didn't know the first thing about running a business. I started off by making films for community projects and stories. Making films suddenly became a big part of my life and it was something I loved doing. It also gave me the chance to free myself to help communities with their fire management as well. With the combination of film and fire, I was able to keep the fire work going across many uncharted places.

But in the end, I simplified my life by just working on my own from home. It was the best way for me to put more time into my dreams and family without the extra baggage or stress. I considered my boss to be the land, Elders and spirit, and worked directly with the people and community from there. That was my personal business strategy that I kept implanted within my heart. All I needed to do was earn enough money to survive, so I could focus on what I loved doing best.

From there the filmmaking work was going well but the fire work eventually started to take up more of my time. I started travelling to help communities with their fire projects in different parts of the country. One of the earlier burns down south resulted in learning more valuable lessons. I went to one of the burns thinking that I was going to work with the Indigenous community. But there was only one person who represented the country and he wasn't really interested in fire in the first place. I soon realised that it was mostly organised by a government land management agency. They took me to a small piece of sand-ridge country which hadn't been burnt for over twenty years. When we got there I waited and watched as other cars and rural fire trucks turned up to attend the day.

Instead of meeting Traditional Owners as expected, there were mainly ecologists, government workers and firefighters there to witness the event. They had about four ecologists there and I couldn't help feeling that they were there to test me out. It wasn't the warmest of welcomes, and being there that day just didn't feel right. The government agency person first started off by telling me that I wasn't allowed to light any fires and that only the trained rural fireman could do that. The officer in charge was then appointed as the leader of the burn and it was time to begin.

First, the Traditional Owner representative was encouraged to start everything off. He welcomed everybody really nervously and then went on to tell that he knew nothing of fire or the landscape. I couldn't blame the guy, though. I think he was dragged there just the same way I was. He then acknowledged me and then handed it over to me to talk about fire. That made me feel even more uncomfortable, as all the eyes present focused on me in a cynical way.

Because I was a little suspicious of the whole gathering I decided to try the reverse approach. I asked the group of expert ecologists to go first to interpret what they knew about the country. I kind of put them on the spot and after a few looks at each other they chose their spokesperson. 'This is a dry sclerophyll forest which seems to have eucalypt and stringybark trees with a number of understory plants. Judging by the plants in this system it is recommended that this landscape should be burnt within seven to ten years.' That was the end of his speech and all the professionals there agreed with each other in a final confirmation of satisfaction. 'Does anybody else want to add anything?' I asked them in a kind and encouraging way. With no takers I was finally left to begin interpreting what I could see from the Indigenous perspective. I huddled them all up and asked them to follow me off the road they were standing on and into the country.

'This is sand-ridge country, because of its sandy, light-coloured soil. This country is considered medicine country, because it has many small plants and grasses that grow in this type of system.' Within about one hour I had finally finished my interpretation, after walking them through the country. We were smelling things, eating things, talking about uses for many plants in that special type of country. Then I showed them what vegetation would burn and what wouldn't burn, the behaviour of the fire and where it would go out. I commented on how sick the landscape was, from a lack of the right fire management.

As I said, the area had not been burnt for over twenty years and it wasn't looking its best. You could walk on the layers of dead grass and it would almost crunch into dust under your feet. There was no sign of green vegetation, and the visibility of fresh regrowth was very scarce. The country had been neglected for so long that it stopped producing many plants that were supposed to be living there. By the end of my assessment we came to the moment of lighting up the country. I looked at the rural fire guy who was in charge and gave him the nod to go ahead and burn. He stood there a little unsure for a moment and then finally said, 'I think we should let Victor light the fire.' There was a bit of silence among the crowd and then I responded by kindly obliging.

I walked into the country to find the ignition point and then I asked the Traditional Owner to light the dead and dry fuel. He did just that and the fire went well and behaved exactly as I explained it would. Western ways are usually the reverse of the way Aboriginal people see the world. The old people will tell you what is going to happen before the fire is lit, while the Western way is to research the aftermath. The old people will apply the action first, compared to the Western way of doing the research before the action. Even the language is back to front. The English language will say, 'Get me some water.' In Awu-Laya language, it's 'Gno parn yo' – 'Water you get'. Maybe that it is why it is hard for each side to understand each other sometimes?

After the burn had finished I walked into the charred country to explain to the group what had happened. They could see that the fire did what it was supposed to do, but they couldn't understand why. I walked them through the ashes, showing them indicators that were predicted before the burn. The ecologists didn't say very much, not even a question. Instead they just stood there, rubbing their chins in thought. The government workers and ecologists huddled together and started talking about what they had just experienced.

They seemed excited at first, but then started talking about how they could possibly do it better. The head honcho then went on to say that I burnt the country using a gut feeling. How can my judgement of applying fire be a gut feeling after I just showed them how to read the country? I walked away in disappointment at what I heard and felt like I was being used.

From that day on I changed the way I would deliver the fire work. I wouldn't do a project unless it was inspired and driven by the community themselves. On top of that, I wouldn't do a project unless I was officially invited by the Traditional Owners and community from that country. If an agency wanted to invite me, then they needed to show that the Traditional Owners were leading the process. Having a community to invite me themselves meant that the project would be successful and culturally safe from the start. But if Traditional Owners are divided and not working together, then that can cause problems in getting community aspirations happening. But most of the time people work it out and things always get on the positive track forward.

I wanted the work to inspire communities to do things for themselves and take charge of their own projects. To get away from agencies running their affairs for them if they could help it. If the communities are not running their own business, then how are they supposed to learn anything and become independent? Let them fall off the horse – they can't learn to ride if they don't.

Part five

Healing country, healing people

Chapter 19

The 'praction'

Learning Aboriginal land management is always best done when it is practised traditionally out on country. To live the knowledge every day by going out on the land, hunting, doing bushcraft, learning about the plants and animals in between caring for every special place. You can't learn properly sitting in a classroom or talking about it. Watching the Elders doing the activities, seeing the process happen before your eyes. Following them as they take the lead in nurturing their land and culture. The best way to learn is to live the land and the knowledge as much as possible.

I remember one of those early days going back to when I was around nineteen years old. I was sitting around in the warm morning sun with all the families in the community. It was the weekend and before I could think of what the day may bring Poppy came and tapped me on the shoulder. I turned around to find him asking me to go for a walk with him through the bush. He didn't ask anyone else in the community to go, he was intending it to be just the two of us. I instantly got prepared with our hunting gear and started to follow the old man. He was already walking towards the bush as I scurried behind in pursuit. He didn't look back even once to see if I was following him. I wasn't sure where we were going or what we were looking for, but I was keen to see what he was up to.

As the old man walked along, he didn't say anything except give some hand signals now and then to indicate his observations along the way.

Most of the time he would be reading animal tracks in hopes of finding a wild pig or some other bush tucker. Other times he would point out some plants and different types of country that had special knowledge attached to it. Every step we took was a learning experience in how to be one with the land.

We walked and walked and walked, all day long. Over rivers and through scrub lands, we weaved through the rugged landscape. I followed the old man until I started to see the sun setting to mark the end of the day. It was then he finally sat down onto a big old log for a small rest. I was happy to sit down and take a break too, as it had been a very long day. I wondered what the old man was thinking and why we were at this place.

There was a moment of silence as we sat there to regather ourselves. I started to wonder how we were going to get home in time before dark. It took all day for us to get to where we were. The old man finally spoke: 'We better go home, eh?' I gave a relaxed 'Yes' in reply, but he stayed seated on the log, silently peering through the trees. 'You go first, I'll follow you', he said. When I heard him say those words I froze. I didn't know the way home at all. I took my bearings as best as I could and slowly started walking in the direction I chose to be the way home.

I nervously took the first few steps I believed to be right and they were the longest I had ever taken. Trying not to look back too, like I was lost or something like that. I got about ten metres only to look around to see the old man walking off in a different direction. I quickly gathered my pride and hurried off to follow after him. Starting to settle in for the long walk home, I looked up and saw something that surprised me. Peering through the trees I could see that the town was only a few hundred metres away. He had walked me all over the country to a point where we were not far away from home at all.

Once again I took it on the chin, I knew that it was all part of learning from him and the country. On the bright side, it was good that we didn't have far to walk home. I smiled in envy of the clever old man and what he had done. 'You need to take notice', he said. 'You need to take notice of everything. If you don't take notice, then you will get lost.' He wasn't just talking about the walk that day either. I got the message that it was the same for anything that I did in my life.

He went on to teach me how to navigate better next time, which was a skill that I would need to apply in any unfamiliar territory. 'You have to praction', he added finally. What he was telling me was to practice what he was teaching me. I didn't dare correct him for the incorrect term of 'praction' instead of 'practice'. Besides, I liked 'praction' better than 'practice', because it has the 'action' in the praction. I loved how the old people used the English language on their own terms. It was always beautiful to hear them speak their own versions of words so confidently.

Over the years I've heard the old man say 'praction' to me on many occasions for many different skills. Every time I heard him say that word I liked it more and more. With the application of praction for many bush skills learnt, I personally came to believe that Poppy's unique word did have its own special definition after all. To me, praction meant applying an action for the wellbeing of people, in a way that is culturally in tune with the natural world. An action that is applied to benefit the country and, in return, benefit ourselves. If the activity does not benefit the country, then it is not praction.

The most important component that guides people through the process of exercising praction is the land. Just like the old man had said, you must take notice of everything on country. The country is where the knowledge comes from. The old man would look at an ecosystem and read all the indicators to determine its health. He would point out the cultural indicators of what the country was useful for and how it was managed. This was a language coming from the country that only trained eyes could see. Applying fire or any other cultural practices to the landscape is done by the country communicating with the custodian.

Reading the landscape is a skill where the land is the boss and tells us what to do. Aboriginal people have perfected this technique in synergy with the environment for thousands of years. Finding a way to help certain communities regain this knowledge and connection was the challenge. Once people saw the value in hosting a workshop on their own country greater benefits were being achieved.

It was great that people could go to fire workshops on other people's country to gain more experience. It is so valuable for people to learn about fire on different landscapes and places. But the most effective way to share knowledge with people is for them to learn on their own country. This way they are able to build on their own knowledge from their own traditional land more accurately. They also learn faster as the dots join to help them see the big picture. It's sort of like blowing the dust off so they can see the knowledge that may have been lost, hidden in the land. Working this way gives the community the support to get fire happening on their country in a much faster and empowering process.

Over the years of sharing knowledge with communities this way, amazing results were being achieved. Some people were starting to see their country through the Aboriginal fire lens for the first time. This was proving invaluable for communities who had lost much of their knowledge and Elders. The land is the oldest living Elder for any Indigenous clan group and has been there all along. The country is our teacher: we learn all our knowledge from the land, waters and skies.

As I mentioned earlier, Indigenous teaching methods are based on knowing what will happen before the praction is applied. When a fire is lit and it behaves the way it's expected to, the land is showing you that the knowledge is true. When the right vegetation grows and animals come back to the country, people can see that the land is showing them this. The land is the leader all the way through, and the teaching and application of knowledge comes from that. It is more like interpreting the country, giving the land a voice through reading the indicators. Once people get the idea, they can be left to continue the praction on their own country. The land will keep teaching you even when the old people are gone.

Getting the young people of today to engage is the biggest challenge for every knowledge-holding Elder to accomplish. But it's understandable when you realise that young people today have so many distractions going on in their heads. Youngsters are different today compared to the youth two generations or more ago. They look at social media more than they look at the country.

Using the video camera seemed to attract the young people's interest to the whole concept of recording the Elders' knowledge. But even then, we had always found it difficult to fully engaging the youth. At first, the process of filming was recording the Elders on camera while the youth sat around and listened. Eventually some of youngsters would get bored and start disengaging from what was going on. Many of them would walk off looking at their mobile phones or start throwing rocks and sticks around the place.

In my mind we needed to try something different to the usual sit-and-listen-to-the-Elder approach. So putting the youth in front of the camera to do the talking and demonstrating started to get them more interested. Getting the young ones to do the action under the direction of the Elders got everyone contributing.

Since then things have never looked back – having the youth playing the Elders' role made an amazing difference. In fact, getting the youth to do the actions for the Elders is how it is supposed to be. The Elders give the wisdom and the younger ones undertake the task of achieving it. The Elders pass on the knowledge and the younger ones learn it by doing the action. Keeping these Indigenous teaching principles as the structure for the fire workshops was a good way to go. On top of that, other young people were watching their own generation stepping up, and that encouraged more to take on the role.

This way we were doing all the essential parts of activating people, country and culture. Everything benefits at the same time and in consideration of each other. When the praction activates everything to move forward together, it becomes living knowledge. If any of the workshops I conducted were not achieving this, then it was being done wrong. Indigenous teaching methods are not only based on what is taught, but the way the knowledge is taught and shared. The process of learning Indigenous knowledge and applying the praction is what triggers greater understanding and connectedness. It is totally opposite to most of the Western teaching we see today.

Our current systems are partly the reason why it is so hard to get Aboriginal fire management back on country. Sitting around talking about the concepts of fire in a meeting room with people gets you nowhere. People can talk until the cows come home about their views on fire and nothing much ever happens. It is hard to get people to understand the country while sitting in a meeting room. There are way too many differences and indifferences in people for that to happen today. The films and practical workshops on country cut through the talk every time and get people listening with interest based on implementing action.

One tool that Western governance systems are based on is evidence in the courtroom. So I figured that the films were a way to become evidence to show them the proof in the pudding. If it is evidence that the Western world understands, then it is evidence we need to give them. Getting the fire happening on country seemed to move a little faster this way. The only problem is that the Western government won't let us burn to demonstrate. So we are stuck in a place where we can't give Western agencies evidence, and they can't give us what we need to provide it.

After a decade of communities hosting little workshops in many areas, the momentum of interest and support grew. Some of the broader community were finally seeing the country through the Aboriginal lens for the first time. They could begin to understand the connection between land, culture and country. Most importantly, they could see how Indigenous fire knowledge can benefit country and people, including themselves. Delivering the fire aspirations this way created a lot of excitement, with more people wanting to learn.

Year after year, one place after the next, I assisted beautiful communities from all over who were trying to advocate for their own fire programs. Travelling and meeting good people wanting to learn and share the same dreams. It's a community network that keeps on growing and has been for a while now. A couple of close friends I consider family would occasionally pull me out of trouble when I had no money. It's something I've had to expect every year due to the uncertainty of where the next pay would come from. But it was the communities that kept everything going, helping out with making little things happen from nothing. They all know who they are and I don't think so much could have been achieved without them.

There were key people from community and other agencies that wanted to support me in getting Aboriginal fire back on country. Some were already interested in Aboriginal fire through their own personal connections, and some simply saw the common sense in it all. Some of them were passionate from head to toe and would come to many of the workshops. Reviving cultural fire practices became the dream for all these good people who were interested, and they went out of their way to get involved.

It got to a point where I was seeing them more than I was seeing my own family at times. They all started to form a team along with Jacqueline and the UTS crew from Sydney. Some of the crew were handy in organising relationships and finding ways of dealing with the Western policy side of things. Their guidance through the government's red tape around fire and safety was essential. Especially for the southern communities that lived close to towns and private properties. It was perfect, because they would help cover all the things that I didn't like to deal with. You know, all that policy stuff, and trying to get us to work within the Western burn plan. I am better at activating traction with the community, working with them to concentrate on putting the fire on country.

I was constantly blessed to meet more great people from different parts of Australia who started to engage with the initiative. I had the privilege of doing workshops with Traditional Owners in Victoria, Tasmania, New South Wales, Western Australia, the ACT and, of course, Queensland. More people got involved from those communities and states and the alliance grew. With the National Indigenous Fire Workshop bringing them together annually, everyone involved built strong relationships with each other. All of them wanting to strengthen their culture by getting Indigenous fire management happening back on their lands.

I was proud of how far the work had come; I had no idea that it would pan out this way. The greatest thing about the Indigenous fire network was that it was all developed from community. It came from the model of community mentoring community. Taking ownership and promoting change from the ground up, driven by the people. It was the only way that it could work: the people doing it for themselves instead of waiting for the government to do something. Having so many people involved from all walks of life showed that it was an Aboriginal-led project for everyone. Without a doubt we are all determined to have Indigenous knowledge recognised in mainstream fire management solutions.

With the growing demands of cultural fire management programs, we all decided that there needed to be some coordination, or an Indigenous-led fire entity. That was when Firesticks was born: an entity to support the praction, help people get their own fire projects happening and build on the networks. In no time community members from the growing network took ownership and started playing their roles in getting Firesticks going. I was blown away by the commitment of the board members who were all made up of community and long-term supporters.

Now there's so many good people involved with the initiative to help it along. The National Indigenous Fire Workshop got too much for me to handle and Firesticks started to manage it from there. I was exhausted setting that up every year and I needed to slow down a bit. The main thing was to get everyone involved so that they could take over what had already been started. The funny thing is that Firesticks didn't have any money to do anything, but it had plenty of community support. It was on its way to build on that, and become more efficient for the communities into the future.

I carried on doing the work in the same old manner; it would be some time before support would be there to help and there was no point waiting. Kept doing small projects with communities back home in northern Queensland as well with fire, the arts and film. I always loved going back home to work and be close to family. Trying to find time to see old TG was always on my mind too. I would sit and tell him about my adventures and share what I was learning from my experiences. He always loved seeing me, but we both missed our earlier times together the most.

I still took the old man whenever I could to close jobs in nearby communities in the Cape. But it was getting harder and he ended up needing full-time care in the Cooktown Hospital. It got to the point where I could only visit him, not take him anywhere; that was really hard. The hardest part was leaving his hospital room after my visit.

But that still didn't stop him from going to the big fire workshop every year. Right or wrong, he was going to go and that was that. We'd put him in his wheelchair and push him through the bush. I would pull backwards over the really sandy and rocky parts. Pulling the wheelchair backwards was like four-wheel drive; pulling it forward was two-wheel drive. It was fun and he loved every minute of being with all those people at the workshop, lighting fires. It wasn't a fire workshop without that old man, and everyone was privileged to meet and share that time with him.

It was coming up to the 2015 national workshop and it was decided that we would have it on the old man's country once more. This time it was to be held at a place called Tenakul. Today the place is known as Mary Valley, which is an old cattle station there that originally belonged to Fred Shepard. It was really hard to transport old TG to the location, but in the end everyone helped to get him there. When he arrived he saw up to two hundred people proudly hosted by his family on their homeland. You could see him starting to glow as the spirit of the country energised his frail body.

That workshop was an amazing experience for everyone who attended and the one that I will remember the most. I will always be grateful that we held the workshop on Awu-Laya country that year. It was meant to be, because this time something amazing happened that was so special to experience. The third night of the event always ends up throwing on some traditional dance and live music. After two full days of running around country doing culture and fire, the entertainment at night was always something to look forward to. After dinner it was time to shake a leg to a big corroboree, and old TG was eager and ready to go.

Slowly and proudly I wheeled him in his wheelchair through the crowd and over to the microphone stand. His old frail hands slowly tucked his pipe away and grabbed the clap sticks I was holding for him. We also prepared an earth drum, which was used for Awu-Laya dance and ceremonies. Traditionally, it was a lot of paperbark rolled up and bound together with string to create a big club. It was then hit on the ground to create the bass in half time to the clap sticks. This time we used an improvised version that made a similar sound by using a stick to hit a rolled-up swag laying on the ground. It still put that nice bass vibration into the dancers' feet just the same, and the local mob couldn't dance without the bass in their step.

We were all set to go. I said to the old man that he didn't have to sing for long if he felt tired. He nodded his head and then the corroboree began. He started clapping those sticks and wailing his amplified voice across the country. First his family came out and danced – Lewis, Dale, and all the kids. Boomp, boomp, boomp, boomp, the thud of the bass, the tapping of the sticks. We took turns playing the earth drum and then going out on the dance ground to kick up the dust. The atmosphere was electric and old TG was roaring with energy. He sang and sang and sang. 'Come on, you fellas, get up and dance!' Everyone there that night could feel the vibe the old man was pushing out and it felt good.

He continued on, singing louder, with the clap sticks going full time in the highest pitch. Tick tick, tick tick, tick tick. I was sweating trying to keep up with the earth drum as he continued to take lead of the ceremony. Any time that anyone looked like slacking off he would yell out to them to keep going. 'Come on, you lot, get up and dance!' Members from every group that attended from around the country started shaking their legs on the dirt dance ground. Then to make it even more special the local pastoralist who was Fred Shepard's son got up and did his little shake-a-leg. Dust was flying everywhere, feet were stamping, and the voice of the old man echoed across the valley's night sky.

'Come on, you fellas, keep going.' Old TG wouldn't stop, it was like he was taken over by the spirits. By now people were starting to become exhausted; we couldn't keep up with the old man. I had never seen him with so much energy. Any other time we danced he would need to take a rest after three or four songs. But he kept going and going. 'Come on, you lot, dance!' He even started to get a little angry at people for stopping. You could see that the country and the spirit of his old people was surging right through him. It was so special for everyone there to witness such an amazing ceremony.

I stood there and listened to him sing the Awu-Laya language songs across his land for the last time. As the dance continued, one of the old man's granddaughters came up to me, excited, to tell me something. That all the family could see Poppy's spirit dancing that night. No wonder old TG couldn't stop, them old people were there too, dancing for him. Such a beautiful thing to experience – old man TG was home, and the family was happy to be on their own country.

It was only midway through the following year when we lost the old man at Cooktown Hospital. He had died on 29 July 2016 and it was expected, as families sat by his side. He really wanted to be on his own country; that was his choice. But the hospital would not allow him to be taken that far over dirt roads in his condition. That was fair enough, but not taking him home to pass was the hardest part of losing my friend and father.

Dr Tommy George was the last speaker of the Awu-Laya language. So much more went with that old man; we had lost a national treasure. But one thing that will continue is the legacy those old people left behind. What those old men have done for so many people has been a true blessing. But with no doubt at all, they will be remembered long into the future. It is up to the young people now and that is what the old people always wanted. Make a road for them, give them the tools and let them take over. That is why it is so important to revive the knowledge, so it can continue to be passed down and practised forever.

Chapter 20

The animals talking

When it comes to the animals, they know the right fire for country. Aboriginal people found the way of applying fire to country that is in sync with the native fauna that live in fire-prone systems. The animals know when the right burn happens, where to go and what to do, with minimal chance of getting hurt or stressed over the event. The way the animals react to Aboriginal fire management proves that the practices have been around for a long time.

The old people told me that the timing for burning stringybark in Awu-Laya country is after the emus have finished their breeding. Nesting in the stringybark country is greener and safer for the emus, rather than the other systems that cure and burn earlier. Managing the surrounding country earlier also creates good feeding grounds through spring, and keeps the stringybark burn contained if fire is applied later. 'Neh Adleeba, arden cha,' the old man would constantly say. It means that the emu is story or sacred, and you are not allowed to hunt him. Awu-Laya people are not allowed to eat the emu, so emus get to roam around like royalty on that land. They love the sandier ecosystems because there is plenty of food, enough food for the people to have shared with the emus for many generations.

As I followed the old man through this amazing place, he pointed out where other animals were digging in the sandy soil to get to the roots of certain plants. 'See that track over there, boy? See where that wallaby's been digging? He's digging out the same root as me, he's looking for that same medicine.' The particular root he was talking about was a medicine for a sore stomach. He said the animals use the medicines like people too, and you could see where the wallaby had chewed off the root. 'He must have had a sore gut, poor fella.' They don't just eat food all the time, they gotta have diversity, they use medicine too. If we don't burn certain country for all the different plants, then there won't be food or medicine for them.

Seeing animal behaviours benefiting from the fire is an indicator that the burn is good. The way they react to the right fire is completely different to a threatening wildfire, where the animals flee or suffer injury or death. Fire cannot be allowed to burn anything and everything; it needs to be balanced in order to benefit all living things and that is what Indigenous people learnt to do. The natural world has evolved to depend on humans to continue the responsibility of regulating fire, which is another connection to reinforce that people are a part of the landscape. The animals depend on us to do the right thing.

The old people would yell out to the spirits in most places we went to on country. To let them know that we were there, and what we were doing on that place. They would sing out before burning the country, to let the spirits know that the fire was coming. It's like knocking on the door to come in, instead of barging into someone's house and then starting to spread fire everywhere instantly with a drip torch. You must apply the fire respectfully and with a proper announcement so everything knows – land, animals and spirit.

Then it is important to light up in one spot and in the right spot so that the fire introduces itself to the land slowly. Allow the first ignition point to burn for fifteen minutes before putting any other fire into the country. The fire starts off slowly, letting out the smell of smoke so that everything will know it is coming. Giving all the animals time to respond to the fire and move to safer areas. Because we don't burn all the country at once, the animals do not have far to go to get to safe ground.

The fire will burn from one spot in the form of a circle, slowly getting bigger as it moves along. The fire burning in a circle gives all the animals a 360-degree escape route outside of the flames. The right conditions of the vegetation curing calms the flame down so that the animals, big and small, can get away. Tiny, little insects of all walks of life would make themselves visible as they crawled out of the grass and up the trees for safety. They know that being in the trees means they are safe, since the right fire will hardly leave a fire scar on the tree trunks. The more insects seen climbing the trees, the more healthy the land. All those insects escaping the fire, thousands of lives saved instantly that are important to the lifecycles and are food sources to larger animals.

Many animals go underground too, and hide under logs or within areas of moist vegetation. In all my years of burning country, I have hardly seen any snakes in our burns except on a few rare occasions. Announcing and igniting the fire the right way is the reason for this. When we burn country we must think of them all the time. When the land is healthy with the right vegetation, the logs on the ground don't burn. The native grasses burn too quickly to light heavy logs. When there are heavy fuel loads and the wrong vegetation, that is when the habitat logs are in danger of getting burnt. The fire will burn in one spot for too long and hang around long enough to ignite the heavy timber.

Rural fire services spend a lot of time putting out habitat logs and trees when they burn country with the wrong fuel loads and timing. If the right vegetation and timing is there, there will be far less burning logs to put out afterwards. On the other hand, Indigenous burning application can be so delicate, light and fast that only the old grass burns. The black ash from the grass is so fine it breaks up into the soil and just blows away in the wind. The animals prefer that fire; they want a fire that brings food and does not destroy their home. Leaving the trees and many plants intact, creating shade and contributing to the flower and seed offerings for the seasons ahead.

There are many animals that are waiting for the right fire to come. They will come to the burn; many different types come and visit us while the fire is happening. Many of them are from the bird family and some come for different reasons. The seed birds are happy because they will get to access all the grass seeds on the ground once the grass is burned. Some of the bigger birds can't get to the seed underneath the dry grass easily in many places. They can poke their eyes trying to get to the seed and it can cause infection for them. But once the grass is burnt they have free range, and fly to the ground for a feed of seed. The fire is so light that all the seeds don't spoil and some seeds are roasted for the birds to eat.

Other birds like the plains turkey and the white ibis come along and walk right next to the fire to eat roasted grasshoppers that plague the bush during fire season. The birds mainly turn up on the open country as they walk along, having a roast dinner of grasshopper that fell casualty to the fire. Kookaburras and butcher birds sit in the low branches in the mixed-tree country above the flames waiting as they seek their own feast. The hawks come flying in by the hundreds at many burns I've seen. If not, then there is at least one or two flying through, hovering over the fire where the heat is thrusting grasshoppers high into the air. Black-shouldered kites, hawks and falcons swoop down in a feasting frenzy, which is so beautiful to see.

After the fire settles, you can see the wedge-tailed eagle and sometimes the sea eagle when close to the coastal river systems. They fly elegantly, high in the sky, waiting for the chance to see what the fresh burn has exposed for them. By nightfall there are many other animals coming in to benefit from the burns. The owl sits in the trees, stalking for movement, and the porcupine shuffles through. I liked visiting the burnt country the next day with the old people because they would read all the tracks of the animals. Curlew tracks, snakes, bandicoots, kangaroos, goannas, just to name a few, that come in after the burn overnight.

There is still lots of organic matter on the forest floor after the cool burns, and still plenty of cover to hide under for the skinks, small lizards and many other creatures. I watch the bush cockroaches and spiders venture back into the burnt country after the fire, and scurry underneath the thin layers of unburnt grasses, twigs and leaves. The black ash is also a luxury for some animals like kangaroos and wallabies. They smell the fire from a great distance and make their way towards the site, knowing that fresh shoots of grass will be coming up soon.

Other introduced animals like the cow and deer also react the same way as our kangaroo. They too smell the fire and have the same expectations of fresh grass and shoots on their minds. They all eventually visit the sites days after the fire to find what they are looking for. The cows, horses, goats and deer also come from fire country overseas; they are fire-wise creatures that come from their own fire-prone environments. That is why they come visit the burnt areas too, but they eat too much and leave bare ground. They are not good to have around Australia, because they out-compete all the native animals. They upset the balance, including pigs and feral cats that put a heavy toll on our natural resources.

When we burn to look after our land and animals, we must control the feral animals that don't fit into our country. You cannot manage country environmentally if feral animals are allowed to trample in and trash it. Traditional burning techniques can be used for improving farmlands for cattle, spelling one paddock and letting them feed in the next. It means that farmers can improve the land for productivity instead of moving on and clearing more trees. The native animals depend on the last bits of forest they have, and the last thing they need is more land clearing. That is why improving the farmlands that already exist is an important outcome to support a better quality of life for our native animals.

Some private landholders use cattle and goats to keep fuel loads down, which works for sure. Overgrazing will certainly stop a fire because there is nothing left on the country to burn. This may be okay for farming properties, but if we use grazing techniques for environmental management then we will see problems. I have seen bushland populated with thousands of wild goats. They ate everything, including the bark off the trees. The land looked horrible and the trees were shaped like mushrooms from the goats eating the bottom of the canopy that was within their reach.

It is so good to burn country knowing that the native animals are aware of what you are doing, knowing that most of them are safe. But there is one animal I have seen in the northern parts of Australia that doesn't know fire very well at all. That creature is a feral animal that goes by the popular name of the cane toad. He is not from this country and he freaks out, even when there is a cool fire. The fire can be cool and slow and the old cane toad will jump straight into the flames. I have seen so many dead cane toads after a cool fire as they have no idea how to respond to such an event. I show people the dead toads after the fire, and tell them why he dies from the good fires. He is not indigenous to this country, he doesn't know what to do, so the fire ends up burning him while all the natives know how to live with the right fire.

There are some native creatures the old people want to burn with the fires, like ticks and lice. Burning the country the right way keeps it clean from leaf litter build-up and long, dead grass that helps parasites to overpopulate. Cleansing the country with fire to keep control of ticks and lice is good for the animals too. No one likes living in a land full of parasites, it is not a fun thing to have buried under your skin. The only tiny insects we want to see are the ones that live on organic matter and plants. A special and important one is the native bee.

It is crucial that we are burning the land the right way to protect the native bee and the flowering of trees they depend on. Burning the grass to activate the white smoke that feeds the trees and helps some to germinate and flower. The honey within all of the flowering plants is crucial to a healthy seed bank and insect life. Protecting the canopy for our native bee population is crucial, and also gives such sweet rewards with beautiful honey. The bees don't like the fire – that is why it must not be too hot to burn the trees. That is why the right fire with the right grass smoke is the best for them: it is not too hot for them and the smoke is cleaner.

Protecting our trees with the right fire is also crucial for other larger animals like the koala, possums and other furry natives. They most certainly don't want raging fire destroying all of the trees. One time in southern Queensland, I was conducting a fire workshop on a farmer's property. He had been putting small burns on his land for a while and was keen to learn more. We went to a place that had a mixed-tree system of stringybarks and gum, and he wanted to know the best way to manage it with fire. As we conducted the workshop with about forty people we then lit up the country as it was the right time to burn. The farmer was keen as there was quite a bit of dry, dead grass smothering the forest floor. The fire went well and burnt most of the dry ground vegetation, ending our workshop with the flames going out at the edge of the system.

The next year I was invited back to do another set of workshops in the region and the farmer's paddock was back on the list to visit. We all turned up at the same site we burnt last time with a similar crowd, all keen for another experience. When I arrived I was totally in awe of the beautiful native grasses and plants that were on the forest floor. The trees were thriving and their leaves were abundant and shiny; they looked so healthy. When we looked up high into the trees, there were four koalas sitting there, sleeping away through the day. They looked so content, we stood there watching them, feeling good about how nice the land looked.

The grass was ready to burn again. This time when we lit the grass it only burned certain places and not the entire forest floor. The fire was smaller and was a lot more relaxing this time round. The fire trickled past the gum tree that the koalas were sitting in, sending the light, white grass smoke up and misting past them. While we watched the koalas didn't make a move, they just kept on sleeping. The older-looking one opened an eye to see what was going on and then went back to sleep. They know the fire and the smoke; they know they are safe. Yet there were still a couple people there freaking out at the sight of the fire burning along. The fire went out again at the different country and everything was good. Managing the country holistically for all the animals is how we must look after those animals that seem to be the most endangered of all. If we make the land healthy, then we look after all of them.

Maintaining the health and diversity of all the ecosystems with and without fire is key to protecting and serving our animals into the future. Burning the country to look after it this way takes more time and effort than any other modern fire management techniques. Practitioners have to get out of the normal habits of working nine to five and getting home in time for the football. It will take dedicated managers to take the time to put in the right burns and management needed for each place. That is what it is going to take if you want to look after the land, water and animals with fire.

Imagine what it would be like if the animals were talking, having big meetings together out there in the bush. Old kangaroos telling Dreamtime stories to their young joeys about how people once lived on the land and looked after it. Saying that Aboriginal people used to look after the country with fire and they never disrupted the land that we all shared for thousands of years. Of course there were animal sacrifices through offerings for food and survival, but the people were a part of the land too. Some animals were honoured and respected in a way where they were celebrated through song and dance. That is the people the animals have known for so long, and have become accustomed to our ways as our own.

But we can only wonder what the animals are thinking about our behaviour as humans today. Imagine the animals having a discussion about what human beings are doing to the country and the crimes against the animal kingdom. Imagine what they would say: What in the hell is wrong with people today? They have gone from living with the land to becoming completely mad. They are going to destroy us all; they are going to destroy themselves. We can only hope that humans hear the cries from Mother Nature, see the signs that they've failed to see in the past. We can only hope that they come back to the land – come back and look after the land for you and me.

Chapter 21

What have they done to the country?

When the First Fleet settled in Australia, everything was here. All the different animals, from birds and reptiles, to marsupials, insects and fish. The white fellas know this because they documented it all in books when they got here. All of the country was beautiful and plentiful of food, medicines and life. The trees were huge, being hundreds or over a thousand years old. Settlers have been quoted as saying the countryside looks like a 'gentleman's park'. When you think about it, it is amazing how Aboriginal people lived on the land for so long and did not destroy it.

There is no doubt that the devastation we see cast across the Australian landscape today has developed since colonisation. From all of my journeys around Australia, the most heartbreaking thing for me is seeing too much sick country. Sometimes I feel like crying when I see so much land devastated and neglected. When the old people die the land will die with them. It is happening whether you believe it or not, and all the signs are within the landscape to see.

In the early days the first thing they did when the settlers came to Australia was cut down the trees. The rumour is that if the settler cut down the trees then they could keep the land. Clearing the land for as far as the eye could see. When I travel by air, it always saddens me to look out of the aeroplane window. Sometimes it's nothing but square chequered shapes of fenced farm paddocks stretching forever across the land. Like the patches on a giant soccer ball. In some places there is not a tree to be seen except signs of dead stumps and logs. Everywhere I go I see the devastation that the land continues to go through today. Some people will cut an old tree down for no reason at all. This will not stop until the disconnected people understand how important the trees are to us and our future.

Many towns I've been to have a rich logging history. One place had a massive log sitting on a train carriage in a park halfway through town. It was at least two-and-a-half metres in width and around six metres long. It would have been even bigger when it was alive, but shrunk a bit over the century. It was the skeleton of a massive mother tree, out in the main street for show. There were information boards showing pictures of men holding massive saw blades, celebrating the fallen giant. You will find celebrations of this type of history in towns all over Australia.

Cutting down the majority of old-growth trees was a big mistake. The big, old trees are no longer there to keep the moisture, provide shade and support the diversity of life. Once the trees had been cut down, the rivers then became polluted and all silted up. The quality of water began to diminish and in some places became toxic. Big corporations sucked up all of the rivers and even took the water we don't see under the ground. Rivers were dammed and the blood flow through the veins had stopped. The land became drier and fires became more regular than in earlier times. Wind and dryness started to affect country that was once lush and moist. All of this helped start the problems we face with fire within our landscape today.

It goes right back to when Aboriginal people first saw James Cook making his way along the east coast of Australia. As soon as the Aboriginal people realised the white man was hostile, the land management stopped. Poppy told me stories that the old people ceased to burn the country when the white man arrived. One reason was that they didn't want to give away their position to the troopers who might see the smoke. They also needed the long grass to hide in, to get away from being captured or massacred.

The other benefit of building up the fuel load on the land was to use fire as a weapon. Fire was used to burn out the settlers when the conditions were right. The old man often took me fishing to a special waterhole in his country where one of those events occurred.

Aboriginal fire practices were taken notice of by the early farmers and pastoralists. But only a few concepts were adopted, which involved the general knowledge of fire around livelihoods and basic hazard reduction. Burning country hot for livestock and land clearing was the main aim, trying to keep country open, with good pastures for farming. The land management of Australia has headed in a direction completely opposite to the way Indigenous Australians had managed the land for so long. The misunderstanding of fire and water is one of the reasons why we are spiralling towards the environmental devastation we see today.

In some places the country looks like an old house that hasn't been lived in for a hundred years. Like most empty old houses, it has been trashed by hooligans. All the windows are broken, the paint is cracked, there is graffiti everywhere, and there are massive holes in the walls. No one is living there anymore, and no one is looking after it. Old tyres, washing machines, mattresses, car bodies and industrial waste choke up many places I've seen close to cities. Little do they know of the toxic smoke that rubbish produces for them to breathe in later when it does go up in flames.

Another major mistake of colonising Australia was introducing foreign animals and plants. The syndrome of weeds alone taking over the country has changed the landscape dramatically. This has created different vegetation to what the country is used to. As a result we get hotter fires when we burn vegetation that doesn't belong in this country. Combining that with land clearing and bad fire management, you get wildfires devastating the landscape.

Since wildfires have increased, the land is becoming less inhabitable for many of our native plants and animals. There are different phases of sickness the country goes through after each wildfire. The first wildfire burns through native woodland forests that haven't seen fire for a very long time. It is common to find fire-dependent ecosystems with twenty to forty years of old, dead grass choking up the landscape. Because there is so much fuel, the fire is hotter than the soils and trees can bear.

The wildfire rages at the wrong time of year, with massive loads of dead vegetation to feed its greed. Everything on the ground is burnt to a cinder, nothing but black, burnt ground to be seen. Most of the trees are all burnt to the tips with the canopy left revealing dead, brown leaves. Underneath the blackened burnt bark, many of the trees are clinging onto life. They cannot breathe without their long, lush branches of green leaves. Many of them shoot leaves out from the trunk in stress, to survive.

Down on the ground the soil is bare and burnt, the organic goodness has been torched and damaged. The heat is so intense that it has stunted many of the grass seeds within the soil. The rays of the hot sun belt down and bake the ground even more as the shade fades away. There is not an animal in sight, no insects on the ground, not a bird to be seen or a song to be heard. A sickening silence, like the country and spirits are in mourning. Sometimes it looks like an atomic bomb just went off.

One by one the dead leaves that were once the canopy slowly fall to the ground. They fall in thick layers right across the surface, smothering the native plant life and making it difficult for these plants to return. What was once a neglected land of native vegetation has worsened to a surface of dead leaves and patches of bare dirt. The combination of extreme heat and suffocation makes it hard for many things to grow. Some grassy woodland country can survive in these leafy suppressed conditions for decades, but it's unlikely to be in a healthy state again for a very long time.

With the lack of animals and plants, the food options have significantly depleted. The flowering and breeding cycle of the landscape has stopped providing for the season. The wildfire has burnt right through all of the ecosystems at once, leaving them all to suffer the same demise. Some places are worse than others because of the different country coping with the wildfire in different ways. But in most cases all of the country is so thick and choked up that the outcome is devastating. Not much can survive on that country for a long time, as the country goes into a coma.

After a few weeks, grass and plants start to grow back in some places but in most cases it is sparse. In country where you could find ten plants within a square metre, it dwindles down to a few here and there, far and wide. The return of plant diversity is very limited and usually one or two native species will thrive and take over the country, from different wattles to tea-trees, grasses and hard woody acacias. Every part of Australia has their particular invasive culprits, while some places share the same bleak conditions.

If it isn't an invasive native, then it is an introduced weed that is invading the land. After the first major wildfire there can be a sea of lantana or an introduced grass taking over what was once native vegetation. I have seen this stretch across the land in many states for thousands of hectares. Slowly taking over the country, taking away the identity of the land. When these invading plants take over a number of different ecosystems, they begin to make them look the same. Turning the diversity of systems into one country of invasive plants and heavy fuel loads.

The hot wildfire favours the conditions for the invasive plants to thrive over the original vegetation for each country. In many places the invasive natives and weeds start to grow so thick that you can't see through the country anymore. A wave of invasive woody understory choking the parent trees to death as they build up years' worth of dangerous fuel loads. Landscapes can suffer in these conditions for decades until the next wildfire comes along.

The second wildfire will usually be more intense than the last one. The country still hasn't fully recovered and the trees are not at their strongest. This time the invasive natives and weeds are there in numbers. They are so flammable that they explode to create an inferno that sucks the flames into the canopy. The whole country ignites, pushing the flames so high in the sky that the trees look like clumps of grass. The heat is so intense that most of the trees explode and die, fire storms begin to rage. There is no way the parent trees can handle that kind of fire. In many cases the only vegetation that returns is one or two dominant species of invasive plants.

After the second intense wildfire, the country is burnt black, torched to a cinder. Nothing but the ashes of the plants and animals that were trying to survive there. The trees look like burnt matchsticks poking out of the ground by the thousands. This time the dead, sickening silence hangs around the country for years. In some places the leaf litter completely takes over the ground, with hardly any native vegetation. In others it has been completely taken over by invasive weeds and natives, thicker than ever before.

One of the worse syndromes of continuous wildfire or bad fire practices is upside-down country. I call it upside-down country because it looks like the trees are upside-down. The long dead branches of the trees represent the roots sticking up in the air, while the thickened mess of invasive plants and dead vegetation on the forest floor represents the canopy. It is the worst case when you see beautiful woodland countries looking like this. Most of the plants and animals that make up those systems are not there anymore.

The regrowth of the particular dominant, invasive plant for each place is so thick that you can't walk through it. Not even a kangaroo can hop through its inherited trails through the land. In the south coast of New South Wales I was working on a property that had a lot of bushland with a thick understory like this. It was the end of the day and I stopped in the middle of a road that led through the property.

All of a sudden a small family of grey kangaroos came hopping down the road towards me. They came within twenty metres of me and then stopped and waited. I was wondering why they were standing there looking at me. I realised that they were wanting to go around me and continue hopping down the road. I said, 'What are you guys doing? You can hop around me through the bush.' As funny as it sounds, they took my advice and did just that. The big male one led the way in front, as his family of four followed behind him.

They hopped into the thick bush of lantana and vines, and started on their way through to go around me. I watched the thick rubble of weeds shake along as they crashed through the wall of mess. They got about ten metres in and then there was a large shake in one place for about a minute. They were tangled up in the brush and couldn't go any further. I then watch the vegetation shake along the same way they came in until they stood back on the same spot in the middle of the road.

They stood there looking at me, pretty upset that they couldn't hop through their own bushland. I stood aside and then they slowly hopped past me, continuing down the road to their destination. Even the animals have to use the roads to get around because the bush is that thick in places. I realised that it was late-afternoon time and the kangaroos were going down the road to go to the nearest farm paddock for feeding.

In upside-down country there is no food for the animals within the thick, scrubby understory. There is also no food in the areas suppressed by dead leaves. There was hardly any grass left in most country around the south coast. The only place where the animals could find fresh grass was the man-made paddocks and private properties. Even after decent rain the bushland still remains the same colour of dead, brown leaves. Nothing can grow through that rubbish, even after a good wet season.

The only places that were green after the rain was the farmers' paddocks. All of the native animals flock to the farm fields and face the danger of roads and rifles. There is simply no other food in the landscape to feed the animals in most places. If it is hard for an Aboriginal Elder to find foods and medicines, then the animals will have the same problem. The next day I drove from the south coast of New South Wales through a national park. As we drove along the road I saw that we were deep in the bush and that there was no development in sight. I had never travelled this route before, but I was appalled at the health of the country.

It had serious problems. There was no sign of grass or small plants, and the land showed severe signs of the wrong fires time and time again. I made a bet with my partner travelling with me. I said that I would give her twenty dollars for every animal she could see on the side of the road. This, of course, included all of the road kill that we came across. But the rules were that the bet would stop when we came to a developed area or farmland. I wanted to prove that there were no animals living in the surrounding bushland.

We drove for almost an hour through the national park and there was not one animal in any form that would win her the twenty-dollar prize.

As soon as we hit the first farm paddock there was road kill everywhere. Different species of dead kangaroos and wombats lay battered and decomposed on the side of the road. You could even lose count in places, because there were so many casualties. All of the animals are concentrated around green open farm paddocks and towns to feed. In many places some animals are practically living in towns. Much of the open country can no longer support the animals with food anymore.

The lack of native foods on the landscape has now become a huge epidemic – it is as bad as all the plastics in the sea. So much country around Australia is neglected and laying dormant in suppression. Humanity has already led many species of plants and animals down the path of extinction. We are not only losing the flora and fauna, but also the country. Losing the diversity of ecosystems is like losing a vital organ from your body. If one is gone, then things that depend on that system start to find hardship.

Having different ecosystems is like having all your different shops. Each place will have certain items you can't buy anywhere else. Just about all the animals, and certainly Aboriginal people, depended on the diversity of landscapes. Maintaining the diversity of the landscape was a big part of Aboriginal land management.

It is true that the Indigenous people of Australia shaped the land. Not only did they shape the land, but the land also shaped the people. You can tell where most Aboriginal people are from due to their features. Not only can you tell by facial features, but also by the build. In simpler terms, the rainforest people were short to get through the rainforest. The open-country people were much taller so they could walk greater distances. It must take thousands of years for people to physically evolve to align with the country they live in. But it takes a short time for the country to reflect the people.

The country reflects all people, whether you are Indigenous or not. In fact, every life form on the planet shapes the country that they live in. The trick is to make your footprint shape the country as naturally as possible. The only way that can be done is being in sync with the lore of the land, sea and sky. So no matter what you do, you shape the land. We all know by now that Westernised practices have shaped the land in a destructive way since settlement. But things got even worse when the conservation laws restricting fire management practices got into the act.

Taking people out of the landscape and effectively locking it up has created the major cause of our environmental disasters. For over a century, wildfires have gradually escalated since colonisation, and more so since the first Royal National Park was established outside of Sydney in 1879. Since then, national parks and conservation laws have escalated in restricting fire from most land users in the country. As an outcome, land has not been managed and the phases of wildfire impacting our environment went out of control. It goes to show that even if you do nothing to the country, you still change the landscape.

Australia has been managed by people for thousands of years; if you lock it up you will eventually get the problems of wildfire. It is sad to say that the conservation laws regulating fire have been a key contributor. Conservation laws haven't really helped with prevention of wildfires or maintaining a healthy landscape. Of course, not all conservation is bad, but there is certainly a good portion of it that has been bad for culture and country.

When you add all of that up, you can understand why things are so bad. Not only is the land oppressed by dead leaves and weeds, but also by the dominant governing systems selling off what isn't theirs. I have met Elders that have eyes filled with tears while talking on this topic. The old people feel this the most, because they know just how much has been lost. Not just for the country, but for the people too.

No doubt the spirits of the ancestors are heartbroken for what has been done to their beautiful homelands. The first thing they would say is, 'What have they done to the country?' You can look around and see every lore within the Aboriginal culture broken, through indicators of desecration. To feel for the country is to feel for your own identity, to know your role on this planet. Indigenous cultures of the world had this respect for country and its absence is clear to see. Look at what they have done to the country. Look at what they have done to our country.

Chapter 22

Healing people with country

Everyone is starting to realise that unhealthy landscapes usually means unhealthy people. It is certainly evident when we look at the health of many communities today that live in a fractured landscape. It goes right back to when Aboriginal people were first taken from their lands and put into settlements. They were commonly seen as primitive savages and that hasn't helped their wellbeing leading up to today. The truth is that the old people were very clever and there is much to be learned from Aboriginal people in healing people and country.

Many people don't realise that there are values within Aboriginal cultural knowledge that are beneficial for everyone. It can't just be Western medicine dominating all the time. Just like there are other ways to look at fire through Indigenous knowledge, there are other ways to look at healing people. I believe it is possible to create a healthier society through having a deeper and more respectful connection to the people and the land.

Understanding how implementing Aboriginal fire alone is healing goes back to the workshops that were conducted for our local Indigenous communities. I experienced changes in people I knew very well, which are obvious measurements of success on a personal level. Just like the old people have always said, the young people need to be connected with the land and culture. That is good medicine for the problems that colonisation has cast upon the people and the country.

After a number of times applying the praction with a number of communities, rapid changes in people became evident. Not only were other people noticing the changes, but the individuals were noticing the difference in themselves. They would say to me, 'I feel different, I feel inspired, I feel spiritually empowered.' Understanding the country this way is cultural and spiritual therapy that gives rise to a clearness of identity, pride and ambition. You could also see people's attitudes change towards others of cultural difference, it motivated happiness and the willingness to work together. When you connect with the country you not only empower yourself, but you also begin to understand other people's circumstances.

On one occasion a woman from a community I visited came up to me and said, 'What have you done to all of our men? They used to be sitting around unhappy all the time and angry at the world. Now they're running around all motivated and excited about getting out into the bush. Whatever you did to them, I just want to say thank you.' I said to her that it wasn't me who made them like that, it was the country. Soon there were many similar stories where people were noticing the rapid changes in their community members and youth in the same way. Watching their people benefiting hugely from culturally reactivating themselves and the landscape.

But it wasn't just the men that were learning – the women were coming on board as well. The fire workshops always had a few women attending, but now the ladies are getting involved in great numbers. Getting the country healthy for the ladies is just as important for their knowledge practices too. Healthy country means more natural resources to exercise all the categories of Aboriginal cultural practice. The fire is crucial to opening other doors of cultural knowledge, through managing the diverse fire-dependent landscapes. Gathering craft materials for basket weaving and accessing bush medicine and foods are two examples of many opportunities.

Getting the children to learn on country too has always been an important part of Aboriginal teaching aspirations. Most agencies freak out at the thought of children at a fire, but not when they are in a safe cultural learning environment. Managing country on all levels should be a thing that children have to learn at a young age. Some countries enforce young people to go into military school. In a perfect world it should be learning about culture and country instead. To be born into a world that is connected and culturally healthy is a start in life that every child needs. The kids are wanting to learn too, which I think is way better than hanging around town or playing computer games. There is a great need to have children's programs at any workshop that involves the wellbeing of country and community.

Having workshops for children at the same time as the adult workshops gives the mums and dads a chance to learn too, without worrying about the kids. It is another important way to get more women involved in the programs. It is always good to see general people having the peace and tranquillity to experience the workshops too. Too many times I have seen parents trying to bring their kids kicking and screaming. That's not good for mums and dads – they need to leave the kids with the other children at their own little workshop.

This is where Aboriginal social management has a big part to play to keep the balance and empowerment going across all ages and genres in the community. Men's business, women's business, and children's business all operating with the same knowledge content at different levels of connection. But let's not forget that we need altogether business too, as the community wasn't separated all the time. Balance in learning, living and growing is a big part of Indigenous social lores, which was important for wellbeing and relationships.

Bringing culture back through the fire was creating much excitement for the communities that were getting involved. Seeing a community culturally happy is the biggest buzz I get out of it all – it is so beautiful and amazing to watch. It would have to be the main reason I keep on going with the work, seeing the community and country glowing in synergy. Transformations in the young people continued happening time and time again. Helping the young people to see their country, knowledge and responsibility is the key. I met a community in southern New South Wales who had two young male rangers who were willing to undertake fire management. The first job was to go to an Elders' meeting to talk about the work that was to be conducted. I asked them if they wanted to film the young lads conducting a fire assessment on behalf of their clan.

The Elders laughed respectfully and said, 'You won't get boo out of those boys. They don't talk at all, even at home.' I accepted their response and said that we would try and see what happens. After the meeting we were soon out on country with the shy young men. It was true, they didn't say anything throughout the first part of the day. Then they began to learn and connect with their country and soon enough they started asking questions. A couple of hours after that, they were presenting their observations in front of the camera. By the time we were ready to put fire on the country, they were talking semi-confidently about what they were experiencing. It was a stark transformation and, most of the time, the land will have a big effect on the young people if they are interacting in the right way.

The method of applying filmmaking to the praction was doing an amazing job of building confidence. Helping people to start speaking up at meetings and taking the leading role in representing their community and country. It was the thing that was missing in their lives: knowledge, country and the praction. Watching the youth gain access to this magical energy was good medicine for the older generations to witness too. In most cases the Elders and families are proud of their youngsters and express it through emotional responses of joy.

I am certainly not saying that cultural burning has solved all of the problems, as there is still much work to do to improve social wellbeing in many areas. But it is certainly a taste of the possibilities to help activate a better future. I am grateful that I have had the privilege to witness such good stories of people healing each other and themselves. From mending relationships between black and white, to easing social problems within the Aboriginal society itself. Casting happiness upon the people helps solve the problems that are in the way of seeing dreams and opportunities. There have also been family feuds and disagreements that have improved through activating wellbeing through country.

For Indigenous people, it's all about connecting back to country and with each other, together. Learning things that some of the older ones never had the chance to learn themselves. They start to realise how much they have missed and how they need to change to make their community better. Some of the bitter ones don't come to the workshops at first, but many eventually do in the end, and that says it all. But in most cases Elders are welcoming of the process with open arms and it is a breath of fresh air and hope. The gratitude of smiles glowing with pride has continually measured this time and time again. It is the medicine the whole community needs; it is the medicine everyone needs.

The land can give a person so much benefit towards their general health in many ways. Firstly, the mind is strengthened greatly through exercising holistic knowledge, and its interconnectedness seems so good for the soul. I was always envious of how the old people's minds were as sharp as ever in their old age. Always on the land, being reminded about all the amazing stories through their relationship with country. When you know how to read Mother Nature culturally, she talks to you all the time, keeping you up to date and in tune with things. Even better if you are keeping the praction activated. Things that are happening with the seasons right now, and indicators that give you purpose and remind you of the stories. Having a strong practical knowledge active on country may have been why the old people's minds were so sharp right through the aged years.

I've seen people improve their health by understanding traditional diets and foods from their homelands. Understanding that their traditional foods are not white sugar, flour and bully beef. The old people always hunted fresh meats, and gathered fruits and vegetables from the country. Fresh gourmet foods from the land is what should be on the menu all the time. The Aboriginal cuisine is a vast range of beautiful fish, animals and vegetables. Things like fresh barramundi, mud crabs, lobsters, kangaroos, turkeys, goannas, turtles and the vast range of fruits and yams, just to name a few. If you live on traditional Aboriginal food, then you will live like a healthy king or queen. Any foods you see on the restaurant menu that are indigenous from Australia is Aboriginal bush tucker.

Some people give up on bad habits as a result of acquiring cultural knowledge from the land. Health is a major reward of reactivating culture and is crucial if you want to grow old to be an inspiring Elder. Walking country and being active is a big part of activating cultural practices. You need to travel from place to place all over the country to deliver the right fire. Walking the country after the fire is also a popular exercise, finding cultural heritage and accessing places they haven't been able to before. The old people walked all over the country daily, keeping fit and healthy as they hunted and cared for the land. It's no secret that connecting to land and culture is good physically, and good for the mind and spirit.

There are many who would agree that activating cultural practices is good for Aboriginal people and the land. There is no doubt that it's good for the mainstream community too. Over time there have been many non-Indigenous Australians that have also positively changed for the better. The magic from the country was giving them an amazing transformation too. There have been droves of white Australians that have come to the fire workshops and have walked away with a different perspective on a country they thought they knew, and an appreciation of Aboriginal culture and knowledge.

When people see the land the right way they begin to think about themselves, who they are and their actions in the past. There have been people who are totally anti-fire who come to one workshop and then walk away with a totally different perspective. A wife of one man came up to me saying that her husband has changed and is very excited. He was totally against fire; now it is all he talks about, running around advocating the good fire to the rest of the world. I have had third-generation elderly farmers come up to me saying, 'I thought I knew the land, but I have been treating it the wrong way all my life.' Some get emotional as they reflect on how much damage they had done in the past – it is a powerful realisation.

Racism is a mental illness, and if people have this condition then they need to be treated. You can always tell the racist ones, you can see the sickness in their body language and eyes. They will hardly say hello to anyone when they arrive and will stand on their own away from the crowd. They watch with frowns on their faces and their arms crossed really tightly. They will usually be leaning on their vehicles, and if there is more than one, they will be muttering amusing remarks to each other to comfort themselves. Most people from their community will come up to me and warn me of them before the day starts.

I always try and include them and make sure that they hear what needs to be heard to fit the situation of the people and place. Pointing out indicators of country and culture that will appeal to them the most, both environmentally and socially. Mediation has always played a major part of getting many communities working together on Aboriginal fire projects. It's crucial that the sceptics see how it involves and benefits everyone, and that they learn something new.

As the presentation moves along, most times their heads will lift and they start taking notice of what is being said. Their crossed arms start to unfold and they show signs of interest. Most will eventually start mixing and talking with everyone. It feels good to see people healing with each other, walking in the same shoes for just a moment or two.

Over the years of travelling to different places and working with different townships and communities, you can see certain traits of health indicators between the people and the land. The more fractured the landscape, the higher chance the community is fractured too. I've taken notice of this from the start, comparing place to place, and it always seemed to be pretty spot-on most of the time. Sometimes it is not the case for a few, but most times it seems to work out that way.

One time I went to another small Aboriginal community in the remote areas of New South Wales. The plan was to do a burn with some of the Elders and the local rural fire service. It was a pretty little place, a small community sitting right on the banks of the Murray River. I got out of the car to meet the rural fire guys and a couple of Elders already waiting in a field, chatting. They intended to burn a fenced horse paddock next to the community. That was the prescribed burning area and there were strict rules to keep it that way. I soon learnt that there had been a lot of trouble trying to get the burn happening in the first place. It appeared that there was one higher-rank guy from the rural fire brigade that was against the burn. He never turned up at all on the day, but apparently had plenty to say on why things should not go ahead.

The rural fire guys that were present were good fellas (as always), and they were the ones telling me about how this guy complained about young Aboriginal people stealing cars and getting up to mischief. That familiar scene, young people in a remote town with nothing to do, and little opportunity. I started to walk off the paddock towards the river to have a look. It was quite a challenge to get to the riverbank as it was choked up with thick, long grass and weeds. As I got to the edge I saw that it was a beautiful part of the Murray River. There was deep running water and plenty of big tree snags that looked like a good place for fish. It was possible to burn it too, as it was gum country right up to the riverbanks.

One of the community Elders shuffled through the grass behind me and joined me in taking in the view of the water. He showed some happiness as he shared fond memories of the river, growing up fishing and swimming as a boy. I asked him if people were still catching and eating fish from the river today. 'No one's been fishing down the river for over twenty years. The reason why is because there's too much long grass and weeds growing along the river, making it hard to access.' I couldn't believe what I was hearing: a community that lived right next to the river, and they can't access it. Everyone was scared of snakes in the long grass and you couldn't find a clear spot on the riverbank.

Maybe that may increase the mischief the kids get up to – they can't even go fishing and swimming on the weekend. The Elder was pretty determined to do a nice burn around the river, and I wanted to help him make it happen. I walked over to the rural fire guys and told them that we have to burn around the river today. They said that it was out of the burn plan and that they couldn't do such a thing. I explained that burning around the river area will improve the community's social wellbeing.

The rural guys understood straight away and then said that they wouldn't say anything if we burnt around the river. Everyone gave a cheeky smile by way of agreement and we started to light the grass. That day we burnt heavy fuel loads around the river beautifully and gave access to the community. The Elders were so happy, there was a huge sigh of relief as they walked freely to the riverbanks. I soon learnt that many people from the community started using the river once again and it brought some happiness to them. We would never have achieved that if we just burnt the run-down, treeless horse paddock. Now there was a healthier river system and a happier community.

Healthy country means healthy community. You hear that saying so many times, but when do we get to fully activate such a concept, when it comes to managing our environment, social benefits must come hand-in-hand. 'Look after the country while we look after ourselves' is what cultural land management practices are all about. Where fire creates happiness and opportunity instead of the fear which ricochets, causing so much disadvantage.

There are so many benefits that will continue to flow if we can all look at the land the right way. Maybe it is possible to evolve Aboriginal cultural values in a way that the broader communities can share. Ultimately, people have no choice but to be more connected with the country. Many non-Indigenous people are starting to realise this, but it should be in a way that respects the original people and culture from that place. It has been amazing to witness so many non-Indigenous people gain a greater cultural and spiritual experience through the Aboriginal lens.

Many non-Indigenous people struggle to connect with the traditions and customs of Aboriginal Australia. The Western-trained mind usually struggles with understanding the logic of the Aboriginal philosophy of country and spirituality. People have been influenced to separate things into boxes for so long that it takes a bit of convincing to see the world in a holistic, interconnected way. Unless they have learned to understand Aboriginal people, it will take a while for most to make sense of it. When I share knowledge with an Aboriginal person, they seem to get it straight away.

Over the years, I have noticed another repetitive trend within the many workshops conducted. There would be an Aboriginal person who has very little traditional knowledge of country, and a non-Indigenous person with the same level of awareness. When a concept of traditional knowledge like fire is shared with both of them, the non-Indigenous person usually takes longer to understand and, occasionally, doesn't get it at all. While the Aboriginal person sees the big picture immediately and has an instant moment of empowerment.

The dots join straight away for most Indigenous people because the understanding of the knowledge seems a lot more familiar. Not only do they understand, but they spiritually grow from one level to another in the moment they take in the information. I sort of look at it as activating the cultural memory that comes from our bloodline, ancestry and homelands. The Aboriginal person's cultural memory is currently estimated at two hundred and thirty years away from being colonised. When we look at other Indigenous peoples around the world, it can be a lot longer. Maybe cultures that existed in places like Europe and abroad can date back to a thousand years or more since being disconnected from the ancestral cultures.

Maybe the cultural awareness for certain people can be buried further away in their genealogy, taking it longer to reactivate. When it does click for non-Indigenous people, they also have positive change from the experience and it is equally exciting to see. Their spirit lightens up and their mood becomes joyful and hopeful. Activating the cultural understanding within non-Indigenous people seems to be what is happening.

It only makes sense that understanding the land the right way is a healing on its own. If only people had the chance to open their minds and allow such practices to filter through to our general society. We would see benefits that will come to influence change in our current practices and ways of thinking. I have met a few people who have been victims of the horrific wildfires, losing houses, livelihoods and loved ones. On occasion I have had the chance to have them attend a fire workshop or two. At first they are nervous when the fire is lit in front of them, but within a short time they relax, with a relief of understanding. They get to see fire in a way that is beautiful and a way that makes it possible to live with it in a positive way. They see how important the fire is for the country and how much the land suffers from the wrong fires.

I am always careful when working with sensitive situations like this, but it is important for people to gain confidence and hope rather than total fear. Before the workshop, the only aid they had received for their trauma was to see a psychiatrist, treating the symptoms in such a way that the patient continues to be isolated from the land. I have met wildfire victims that continue to live in fear years after their encounter and become nervous whenever they see smoke on the horizon. I am not saying that Western treatments are not effective, or that we don't need them. I just think that learning about the land gives people understanding and hope. There is a greater opportunity to assist these landholders with programs to learn how to burn and live safely with the land.

There is no doubt that connecting people to the land from the depths of cultural knowledge is beneficial in many ways. I have shared the outcomes with so many people since the beginnings of this work. I am not the only one who can vouch for the fact that activating cultural understanding of country through natural lore is healing. The journey since Indigenous fire management workshops have been made available has brought so many people together holistically and respectfully. Ensuring that the community is involved in cultural land management programs is key to ensuring that the benefits can be enjoyed into the future.

When people come to the workshops and learn about the scale of mess the country and community is in, they freak out. They begin to ask questions like, 'Where do we start?', 'Is it too late for us to get things right?' I believe that it isn't too late to start healing the country and ourselves. To move things in a positive direction, no matter how bad things may seem. One small project at a time with everyone supporting each other is all it takes to get things rolling.

Yes, of course some will try and smear the good work through social media, distort the news to make good intentions look bad, but we must prevail. Activating happiness through applying the praction is all we need to focus on. One little project at a time, over and over again, until the seed grows into a beautiful tree. I think the majority of humanity will agree that change is needed right across the board if we are serious about dealing with the problems at hand. But we are deep in the era of healing and have a way to go before we are maintaining balance with the land and ourselves.

Chapter 23

Healing country

When we look at all the damage done to the land and sea, healing the earth is going to take a very long time. That is if we start looking after it right now. The bad news is that it takes much longer to fix some things than it does to destroy them. Since colonisation, the damage to the Australian landscape is currently well over two hundred years deep. If we activate the country the right way, many small problems will heal quite quickly while other conditions will take twice as long to heal, and some even longer.

An easier way to look at it is: it will take five hundred years before there will be five-hundred-year-old trees in places where they were previously destroyed. A thousand years for a thousand-year-old tree is even harder to contemplate. It will take generations of continuously looking after the land to reach those long-term goals, starting from now. This also includes healing our rivers and oceans, rehabilitating land and reviving our animal kingdom.

We are leaving our future children with an accumulating debt of environmental mess. If we are serious about transforming to reach those goals, then we must start handing down good knowledge and practice to the future children. That means doing what Aboriginal people have done since the beginning of their time. Handing down knowledge in a way that is accurate, sustainable, cultural, and is continually practised for generations. That is what it is going to take if we are going to be serious about healing our planet.

The healing knowledge using fire for the land comes from the same knowledge of maintaining country with fire. Healing the environmental problems becomes far more possible if you understand the land through ancient knowledge views. Knowing the values and indicators of each ecosystem allows you to work out ways to adjust the fire management to improve the condition of sick landscapes. Burning outside of the normal times you would burn the country, depending on its identity and condition. The health status of a particular country determines the best possible application of fire. It's sort of like being a doctor for the land, giving a diagnosis and then the treatment.

There is not one answer to applying healing techniques using fire across all of the conditions of damaged country. One application might work well for one particular ecosystem while results are not as positive for others. Applying fire to an unbalanced system can change its application each season until it becomes healthy. The fire application will shift as the country improves, which is why adaptation of fire techniques is the key to effective fire management. You have to be on country, reading each particular place in person. Sharing indicators of Aboriginal fire knowledge gained through lived experiences is the only way I can explain this chapter. I will try to present this information, in hopes that it continues to be helpful, adaptive and relevant for time to come.

Before settlement, the country was cared for and many ecosystems of the same type would have been at similar health levels. Today, we have multiple ecosystems of the same type that usually have different conditions of health. For example, this gum-tree country has all lantana; this gum-tree country has nothing but leaf litter; this one has just suffered a wildfire; this one is full of an invasive native; and this one isn't too bad, with lots of native grass and plants present. When the country has different conditions of health, you need to be able to apply fire in different ways to activate the country the best way possible. It's the same for people too: if one has a lung problem, the other has a heart condition, and this fella has a physical injury, you wouldn't give them the exact same treatment.

Firstly, it is important to know what country should look like and what kinds of plants and animals are meant to be living there. That is where the knowledge of bush foods and medicines is extremely important. Knowing which plants and animals should be there, and the indicators to bring them back. Some country will take a long time to heal and some will return good outcomes from the very first burn. A quick turnaround can be one to five years, whereas others will take decades or more. This excludes bringing back the old-growth forest and many rare animal species, of course. For long-term indicators of success to come back, we need to start making the short-term indicators of health happen.

When some country types are sick, fire needs to be applied more regularly in some cases, unless it is a no-fire country. Fire-dependent country may need frequent burning on different levels, to help it get back to health. If a country is full of invasive weeds and has very few trees, then it may need fire every season until it gets to the point of good health. There are many examples where this has been applied and been effective. It has also been a strategy that Poppy has used when healing Awu-Laya country over the years.

In an area in southern Queensland, the Aboriginal rangers had a property handed back that had been cattle farmed for over a hundred years. The land there is full of introduced African lovegrass that has taken over the property completely. Big, open fields of cleared land and lovegrass, which is one of my most disliked introduced grasses. Because there were no trees, the rangers started to walk around in the thick of it and dig down to the soil.

The soil can tell us what country it is and what trees should be there, to help us find the right timing. One ranger dug up light, sandy, grey soils and that told us it was bloodwood country. In other places they dug up a darker soil, which indicated gum trees. The knowledge of soils told us what trees would reshoot and what time or condition we should burn in those different places. Creating the right fire can involve modifying the usual timing to suit the burning of foreign vegetation. Once we got the first fires in, we started to see results straight away.

Trees started to pop up where expected, and native grasses began to shoot again. Having a few good indicators coming up after that massive fuel load was removed was just the beginning, knowing that there will be years of work to do. In this case, it was advised to burn every year from here on until we see the signs to do otherwise. The African lovegrass is very stubborn and doesn't mind fire; it will reshoot and dominate again. Its long strands of tussock grass blades will soon grow to fold over and smother the native plants once more.

Being a tussock grass, the plants' root bases are far apart from each other, which creates spaces of bare dirt between them. Burning every possible season makes sure the exposed ground is always made available for the natives to take hold. Burning often to make the fires become cooler, to keep the invasive fuel down, and to help more of the native species compete. Leaving the country for more than two or three years will result in creating more of the wrong fuel loads. When it burns again, it will create hotter temperatures to favour weeds and invasive natives.

This technique of applying the fire every year in the early healing stages means it will eventually burn less and leave more green vegetation behind after each burn. It will start to form its own mosaics within its own system. What doesn't get burnt this season may burn next season. Little areas of green grass and small ground plants still remain, leaving areas for the wildlife. Only burning what needs to burn, to keep the invasive vegetation down and stop it from seeding. I've seen cases where we were burning just the African lovegrass while the natives in-between were too green to burn at all.

The frequency of seasonal burns helps to nurture the young trees until they grow high enough to get out of reach of fires that are too hot for them, giving them a chance to shoot up and establish themselves without being stressed by a wildfire. The trees are up over two metres now, and on their way to becoming adult trees in years to come. The aim is to re-establish the trees over many years until there is canopy back to provide shade. Trees also help provide the right conditions for many native plants, and some won't grow unless the trees are there.

The shade also helps get rid of many introduced grasses and weeds, but unfortunately not all of them. Bringing back the trees is to bring moisture and coolness back onto the country. More shade means we have a chance of having more moisture and some invasive plants from dry climates don't like too much moisture. It will be a long hard fight to get rid of introduced grasses like the lovegrass, but continuous efforts to bring back the natives will help out in a big way. There is a long way to go with these types of changed landscapes, but persistence has led to positive results.

Within a couple of years of burning annually, there were native grasses starting to appear everywhere. Weeds like the balloon cotton that were high in numbers had dwindled down to just a few. Black-headed spear grass, native couch and kangaroo grass were populating themselves throughout the soils in-between. There were native herbs of all sorts littered throughout and this was the response we were expecting. The young rangers were sharing the successes together and spoke on camera to make their film case study. At least five years had passed since then. I revisited the site and found that a couple of years of burning had been missed. Busy schedules and constant training programs were leaving no dedicated fire rangers full time.

There had also been a hotter burn that occurred three years before, and weeds were riddled throughout the system once again. I was pretty disappointed, but took it as an example to educate the crew. By the end of it we decided to burn, but as expected with so much fuel, it was a little too hot. We lost a few young trees, but managed to keep most of them, and it was a good lesson learnt on not following up on the frequent burns. It is another example of why we need Indigenous fire managers full time on country, always nurturing the land. If we leave the land to rebuild fuel over many years, the next careless application of fire could set the land back dramatically.

What needs to be considered is that the country now has two seed banks within the soil. There is the native seed bank and introduced seeds laying dormant in the soil, waiting for their preferred conditions. It is possible to burn for the natives in a way that the introduced seed bank will not shoot favourably. I have seen this result many times around the country with a number of introduced weeds. When you burn at the right time for each country, you favour the native seeds from that system.

Luckily Mother Nature gave plants different tolerances for different heat for germination, otherwise they would all thrive in the same conditions. The hard part about the seed story is keeping the right burns happening on country all of the time. Some seeds can stay in the ground for up to a hundred years and some hopefully a lot less. But it boils down to the challenge of killing off the introduced seeds through burning the right way constantly, to ensure natives dominate. It only takes one wrong fire and the introduced or invasive native plants will rise once again. To put the country in balance there needs to be flexibility in applying the traditions of good fire management – otherwise the natives will lose.

In the days of managing country with Poppy and old TG, we treated weed-infested country right from the beginning. For years we kept burning the same places over and over again, until there were hardly any weeds in many places. Always applying fire here and there throughout the fire season. When the old people passed, we left the country alone for a while in cultural respect. We left it for two years and then we came back to start putting the fires back on country once more.

I returned with Poppy's grandson Lewis and we were heartbroken to what we came back to see. The land had been torched and fire scars were up high, near the canopy. I am not going to mention how the fires happened, but the beautiful country achieved by the old people was counteracted with weeds and invasive wattle littered throughout many places. The country was set back once again, and there was nothing we could do except try and move forward. Patience, patience, patience, with persistence, is what is needed to get rid of the weeds.

When we look at defeating the weeds it is important to put all of the focus on the natives. So many people make the mistake in life of focusing on the problem instead of the strength of our original self and wellbeing. The same thing goes for the country: don't focus on the weed, focus on the natives. When we manage the country for the natives, then we favour them to outcompete the weeds. The land has an immune system, just like us, and when we activate it to make it strong, it will fight the causes of sickness. But the land needs people to connect this way to activate the process, especially in fire-dependent systems.

Another big problem is the weeds that stay greener longer than the curing of the native grasses. If late-curing weeds take over an ecosystem, then the country will miss out on the right timing because it can't burn at all. Weeds like Paterson's curse, and Wynn cassia, can stay greener longer and completely take over the system. If there is dry fuel there, then burning just on the edge of early winter after the first couple days of dew can get the first fire happening. The fire might not burn everything, but it will kill off a lot of the weeds. A follow-up burn can be done within a few weeks to burn off the rest, once it is dead and dry. Walking through the system to light the leftover weed patches is the way this is done.

If there is nothing dry to burn, then chopping off the tops of the plant with a blade and letting it scatter and fall to the ground around the weeds leaves more dead fuel to help support a fire. This work is done in the off seasons of fire, so that the fuel will dry and be ready for the time to light. Otherwise, you simply have to wait for another season or two for the dry fuel to build up, if it looks like heading that way. But in many cases you need to get the job done earlier, to prevent the problem from getting worse. Landcare groups have assisted some projects by preparing fire grounds this way. Ready for a fire practitioner to come along afterwards and apply the burning applications.

Most modern land management practices will fight weeds with poisonous chemicals before they try any traditional-based bio techniques. I always favour not using any poisons at all unless there is drastically no other choice. We need to get the foundation of our fire management right before we resort to the spraying of poisons. Allow time to apply the right fire management over a number of years before chemicals are used. Give the country a chance to show the possibilities of healing first, through traditional fire applications.

It is possible to apply the fire first in most cases; most times it will create a better position to deal with the problems at hand. After applying the right fire a number of times, the weeds usually end up being a small patch here and there. You could probably pull most of them out by hand in the end. I have seen continuous use of fire settle the weeds down to just a few, many times. Of course there are a few hardheads that are more challenging, but in most cases I have seen success.

Another horrible category of weeds that grow in the no-fire country are the ones that grow in our waterways. The culprits that choke up the river systems, disrupting the quality of our water and the life it supports. This includes weeds that grow in all types of no-fire country. The only way to get them out is with harvesting techniques. You certainly shouldn't be poisoning the no-fire country weeds with chemicals, especially when it comes to our waterway areas.

Fighting against the weeds and invasive natives in no-fire country points to using other forms of practical labour. What is wrong with employed teams wading down the shallow rivers, cleaning them, and pulling out the weeds and rubbish? It will certainly improve the quality of the waterways and allow healthier river systems for wildlife. Keeping them clean will also improve the chances of there being less fire hazards in the dry times. The weeds in the river systems can build up so much dangerous fuel around the parent water trees. We must protect those trees and the water at all costs, and it should be a major focus.

We must protect all our trees and allow them to reshoot and head towards old growth forest once again. When country has been cleared of the trees the land dries out. Protecting the trees can also assist in drought times for many of the plants and animals. Trees are also important to attract water, including rain. It may not be proven in Western science, but it is something I know is valid through traditional knowledge. The trees are connected to the sky and we must not think otherwise as they sing for rain like many animals, plants and cultural songs do. I have seen times in cleared land areas where the clouds were only raining on all of the patches of small stands of forest left.

Fire is an important tool to grow many trees back on the land and activate the seeds laying waiting in the soil. When fire is applied on the soils the right way, the parent trees can start shooting again. The good thing about growing trees with fire is that the right trees pop up in the right country. The other advantage is that you don't have to water the trees as they will look after themselves. I am not against the endless efforts of tree planting, as it is great to see people plant rainforest corridors, re-establishing ecosystems. But I think in fire-prone country we can improve the rehabilitation by activating the land. In some cases the land has been farmed and tilled so much that we may need to grow trees by hand. I have seen a good Aboriginal friend of mine doing that on a hundred-year-old sheep-ridden property in Western Australia.

My experiences of applying fire to cleared landscapes result in the parent trees growing themselves from the right fire. If we follow this the right way, we will be able to save a lot of effort and money by activating the land to grow its own trees. If we can get this right, then land care groups can be introduced to activities without wasting time, money and energy. When a place is treated with an application of fire, there will be follow-up work needed, with activities other than burning country. Which now brings me to a really important Aboriginal land management practice based on harvesting and utilising plant resources: the harvesting of country.

Harvesting country is a diverse practice based on Aboriginal people using the plants and animals in a way that both regulates them and helps them thrive. As mentioned before, Aboriginal uses of plants and trees are done without killing the plant. Even tubers and yams have the end of their shoots reburied into the soil. It is lore not to leave dug holes open and exposed – you must cover them up again, shifting and loosening the soils, leaving the ground ready for the food source to reshoot again. Even currants or berries that come from some trees are picked by breaking off the branches, like pruning. The old people told me this was done for certain plants so that they shoot even more with better fruiting next season.

Small invasive plants like wattle and other understory species were used for multiple reasons. The small plants and understory growth assisted in keeping the country clean and in return it serviced the needs of the people. The country has been providing for the people for thousands of years and it will continue to flourish if we use it properly. That is why traditional lore based on using the country through harvest or hunting was strict and abided by. There were seasons to hunt and gather using sustainable practices reinforced by traditional lore taught from the country.

The country loves us when we fit into the divine beauty of being a part of it. The old people would sing to the country all the time, through songlines and dances. Old TG would talk to the country and let everything know that we are about to apply the fire. It's just like when people talk to their plants at home – some say the garden grows better as a result. The practices of using the resources helps to regulate country too. The harvesting of country was an important contributor to regulating the balance of the vegetation throughout the country.

Every plant has single or multiple uses, whether it is indigenous or not. Even the weeds hold beneficial values, as our natives do. There are weeds with strong medicinal properties, or that are a healthy vegetable, or a useful implement, or that have a great smell. Some can create amazing oils and I have even heard of weeds being used to create bricks for building modern houses. If we make a good effort to improve the understanding of selective harvesting of country, there could be some amazing outcomes. It could help sustain jobs to keep the land cared for at the same time; down the track it could bring opportunities that may change the way we farm.

Imagine the plagues of lantana, carefully harvested out of the land in the revival of native bushland recovery. Using the lantana for making some amazing building product, and by chance it actually does so well that they run out of lantana growing wild in the bush. Imagine that. What if it then started to replace other crops that use too much water. Nothing wrong with dreaming about solutions that could be right there under our noses. It would be great to see more people exploring the harvesting opportunities around invasive plants that are dominating unbalanced country.

The important thing to remember is that we don't want farming machines out there ripping up the land. They would compress the soils and make a huge mess of the country. The noise they would produce across the bushland would be disturbing for the native residents. On top of all that, the last thing we need is machines taking over jobs and cultural responsibility. We need to maintain old values if we are to reap the full benefits of reviving culture and applying traditional knowledge back onto landscapes. There is too much evidence out there already that supports the greater health benefits in people reconnecting with culture and their environment.

The Githabul rangers in the Kyogle region of New South Wales have a massive eucalypt dieback problem on their country related to an increase in the numbers of bell miner birds, also known as bellbirds because of their high, bell-like calls. It is a situation where a native lerp or psyllid feeds on the large eucalypt trees. The bellbird is a honey-eater species that lives within the outskirts of the rainforest and can nest in the open woodland country. What supports them to nest in the broader open dry forests is the introduced lantana, which creates good habitat for them. In much of this eucalypt country today, there is nothing but lantana smothering the landscape for as far as the eye can see.

The bell miner birds live together in high numbers and they swarm the dry land forests. They are quite territorial and hostile to the other native birds and gang up on them to drive them away. Other native birds that live in the dry land forests would eat the lerp, but the bellbirds keep them away. The bell miners feed on the lerps, but not effectively enough to keep down the population. This increases the impact of the lerps that slowly kill the massive eucalypt trees or make them very sick. Slowly the problem has spread over decades to leave thousands of dead trees, with nothing but lantana dominating the forest floor.

Researchers have been studying this for decades and a solution is needed to deal with the problem of the bell miner. The Githabul rangers wanted to do something about it and fire came into their thoughts. In 2013 they invited me to their country to help them find the right application of fire. When I arrived they took me out into the thick of the problem where there were hundreds of bell miners flying around everywhere. I looked at the evergreen lantana and realised that there was nothing but bare dirt underneath it. That made fire impossible to implement, as there was nothing to burn to kill the lantana.

The rangers had already started to attack the sea of lantana by cutting a track through it with brush hooks. As they slashed their way through, they then applied a quick spray of poison to kill the rest of the plant. It was one of those cases where poison was the last resort and they felt bad using it. But they thought they had no choice, to tackle the mammoth situation at hand.

They also trial-burnt a small patch of the dead lantana to see what would happen. What the rangers showed me and the knowledge we shared soon put us on the right track. I looked up at the swarming bellbirds above and suggested lighting a single test fire to see how the birds would respond. The rangers put a heap of dead lantana together and lit it up to create a flame that danced at least four foot high. When they did, the high-pitched ding-like call changed immediately to a more stressful sound. You could tell straight away that the bell miners hated the fire as their introduced weed habitat went up in flames.

'There you go,' I said. 'You're already on the right track. Kill the lantana then burn it to chase them bellbirds back to where they come from.' Then the native birds that belong to that country could come back and help sort out the lerp. There is a good chance the smoke would help with calming down the little critters too. With the knowledge of burning in that type of country and soil, we were certain that we could activate the native seed bank again. At first the rangers were a bit reluctant as the lantana was plentiful, making the fuel load look a little scary. But I assured them the dead lantana was not so flammable at that time of year. The fire would go out when it hit the untreated lantana – and that's what it did. The rangers relaxed as they could burn the dead heavy fuel loads as cool as possible, without it raging out of control.

Off they went, setting fire to the lantana, creating an even blanket of cool fire across the open ground. They had begun the lifetime task of slowly burning away the dominating weed. Fighting a sea of lantana during the off seasons through summer, then burning when the fire season comes. As a short time passed by, the rangers could see the native vegetation that belonged there starting to shoot again. Trees, grasses, herbs of all sorts, making their way back to freedom. The sounds of kookaburras were starting to return and the process was just beginning. The Githabul rangers like slayers cutting away at the sea of lantana, while the native vegetation reshoots and follows them behind. Bringing back the country that had been there for so long and supporting the animals that depend on those ecosystems, to reclaim their land.

The rangers were excited and they done so much work to get the mission started. The problem was so large that it may take a couple of generations to get through it all. But then a guy from a government agency came along with a bulldozer and he started to tell us how to do things. He then drove his bulldozer all through the lantana to create a firebreak right around where we were burning. The fire could not go anywhere and I knew that was the case one hundred per cent. He drove that bulldozer all over the burnt country, ripping up the ground, and I could only stand and shake my head.

The peaceful work of healing the land had been rudely interrupted. In the end, the involved parties found out that the rangers were using fire and then, with a complication or two, the work stopped. The Githabul had the solution happening and it could only improve with further application, persistence and support. I was excited that Githabul had an amazing project that could boost their community into meaningful cultural work, but it wasn't the case for now. But putting aside the usual scenario of dealing with misunderstanding, there are some important indicators that need to be shared from this story.

Spreading the cuttings of lantana or any invasive native or weed across the bare dirt will create something to burn. If there is no fuel to burn, then doing this is an effective way to create the first fire back on country. It is important to never heap the cuttings of any vegetation into piles. There is no native animal that creates large piles of dead vegetation and logs to create a nest. Yes, the scrub turkey does it and the saltwater crocodile, but they live in no-fire country. If the animals did that in fire country, then their nest would burn so hot nothing would grow in its place for a long time.

Some agencies have a bad habit of pushing all the discarded trees they cut down into a massive pile. When they burn, they create so much heat that you find large circles of bare dirt littered throughout the land. Some have said that the ecologists tell them to do that because it is good habitat. I tell them, 'Show me an animal that creates that pile of mess for them to live in.'

It's not good to pile cuttings and debris up in the bush. Either take it away completely or spread it out evenly. For one, it looks ugly and when the massive pile of logs does burn, it creates too much heat, which produces a white ash.

When burning country with the right application and the right vegetation, white ash should hardly be present. Black ash is the sign of a cool fire and that is all you should mainly see after burning country. It is easier to ensure the black ash if the country is healthy, with the right plants. White ash comes from campfires where heat is concentrated and extremely hot. White ash is not good to see across the landscape, as it is more likely to have weeds or invasive plants reshoot afterwards. But with the first burn on country that is full of introduced weeds, you can usually expect more white ash until it improves next time.

Black ash is good and is the layer we want to see being watered back into the soil with the dew and rain. The native grasses produce the best black ash and it just blows away into dust in the end. It is so light that it sits on top of the ground nice and loose, leaving air to flow underneath. The fires that are so light and elegant create the ash like this, and is partly why there is no evidence of megafires in Aboriginal occupational history. The white ash will create a heavier blanket over the cooked soil and goes hard once it gets moist. I have noticed some fungi-type species growing back on this, but mainly unwanted plants are favoured, or none at all, for a long time.

It is good to understand how to burn most heavy fuel loads as cool and safe as possible. It all boils down to the knowledge of flammability for different vegetation types within their seasonal timings. It is amazing how Mother Nature has made different plants flammable at different times of the year. We would be in grave trouble if all plants were at their most flammable all of the time. The only time most plants are equally flammable is when we are in the middle of a drought summer with a land full of fuel.

Within the fire seasons of Aboriginal knowledge, the flammabilities of all plants on the country varies. Most plants that don't belong to a particular fire-prone system are not as flammable when the native grass from that system is ready to burn. In most cases at present I am slightly adjusting the timing a little earlier or later to create the right fire for what vegetation is going to burn. Earlier or later from the usual right timing to ensure that the burn is cooler and to make sure it even burns at all. It allows the right heat to be applied to look after the soil and support the natives more, even with the uninvited guests dominating.

There will be flare-ups where large clumps of dead weeds and grass are concentrated. But then the fire settles down once it is burning the correct vegetation again, knowing that the neighbouring systems are not ready to burn, or are already managed, and will keep the flames in its intended place. It may take a while for people to gain confidence to practice this. That is why people need time to learn firsthand. It is dangerous burning country that hasn't been managed for so long, not just for people but more so for the environment. People need to be skilled in knowing how to deal with the diverse fuel loads.

The trick is getting the first fires happening on country that hasn't been managed for so long; they are going to be the hardest. Managing country after the first burn or two becomes easier; it's easier to apply a better fire next time. There becomes a greater balance of living vegetation among dead debris as well. The first burns will occasionally need other forms of labour in preparing the country before the fire is reintroduced. The parent trees will usually have large deposits of old dead bark, grass and debris around the trunks. They can burn too hot for the tree and the flame will stay around long enough to create a great disadvantage or death. If the fire gets in and burns the habitat trees from the inside, it usually ends badly and becomes a hazard to manage.

Situations like this lead to teams raking around the base of the trees to clear them from the threat. The highest priority is to rake around the oldest trees and the important larger ones in between. If there are many young parent trees too close together, then don't clean around some if thinning them is needed. After the first burn, you shouldn't have to clear around them again, if the timing of fire is applied the right way. But always keep in mind to clear large amounts of debris away from the mother trees. It's good to give them a quick look-over at every fire, just to avoid the odd casualties even from the coolest of burns. It's always nice to pay the big old trees a visit.

If the country is choked up with dead leaves and has been sitting that way for years on end, the first fire will be long. Leaves burn slower than grass and the smoke is not the best quality. Thick leafy rubble commonly stretches across a number of ecosystems and creates one big system of mess. On the South Coast of New South Wales, some young Yuin Traditional Owners were conducting their first fire cultural reintroduction on country. The boys ended up walking with the fire for thirteen days, until it came to its end. It had burnt around three hundred acres in that time. Other fires I have known can burn cool for a month or more, just to get that thick suppressing layer off the surface.

It is obvious that when country is looking this way, the fire will burn for many days. You have to make sure that reading the surrounding country is done, to contain the fire through different measures. The risk in burning this way is to ensure that the fire does not burn through to warmer temperatures and get out of hand. Making sure you know the points in country to help contain fires ensures the longer burns can be managed safely. Burning these fires at a time where two or more months of winter is yet to come is the best way to avoid problems. If the winter is too dry, then at least burn a section of it where there are manageable breaks.

When applying the first fire to country this way, it is a fire that should not be used to judge how the fire will behave next time. It is a fire that will be a little hotter, last longer, and the smoke will be darker and intense. This is expected with the first burn on country that hasn't been managed in a long time. In time, the qualities of the fire and smoke will improve; patience will reveal these indicators with the right fire management.

First the country needs to be reset, taking out the plants and rubbish that shouldn't be dominating the country, and trying to put the right plants back into balance. It can take two or even three seasons for some unbalanced country to get a good return of native vegetation. It all depends on the country and the problem at hand.

This is where the right fires for each ecosystem will be bad for the plants that should not be there, or should not be as dominating. It's like traditional lore for people, where one fella can't take over another fella's country. If the visitor plays up in another person's country, then the mob send him back to his own country. The same lore is for the plants: the invasive native that should not be dominating the system needs to be sent back to their own country. For the people version of this comparison, they use the spear to chase the person back. In the case of plants taking over another plant's country, it's fire. The fire that belongs to that system is the spear to use. So a boxwood fire will get rid of the invasive tea-tree in a way that kills it and thins it out slowly.

This method has been successful for many invasive natives, like a few of the wattle species, tea-tree species, acacias, casuarinas, and the hard woody types that come from the rocky countries. These all fit into the category of being flammable plants, and the plants you don't want to dominate certain systems at all. Many of them come from no-fire country, but they love to grow in places where hot fires have taken place. They are funny characters in a way, because they are upside-down and back-to-front to the other fire country plants.

They love the hot fires but they hate the cool right-timing fires good for other systems. The right fire will kill them, but they won't ignite completely and burn away to nothing. They are not so flammable at that time, so they don't combust into a ball of flame and go crazy. Instead, they die and leave behind their skeleton of dead twigs sticking out of the ground. The native grass that shoots back creates the right fuel for the next fire that will burn away the skeletons slowly until they are gone. There will still be lots of leaf litter on the ground from the invasive natives as well. This will also add to making the next burn happen, until it improves in future burns.

The invasive plants hate the right fire, but it will only affect them if they are in reach of the heat of the good burn. The right fire for a system will kill an invasive native that is up to six foot tall, or at eye level. After that, they can be out of reach of the good fire and then it is a case of cutting or harvesting them out if they are gone too far. If you let these invasive flammables roam unsupervised for a long time, they will get to the point where only a hot wildfire is supported by their existence.

These are the plants that thicken the mid-storey of the country, and explode into flames that push the fire well over the canopy to the point where trees can suffer and die. That is why we can't let them take over the country; they love it when people don't look after the country. It allows them to thrive, take over, and then create the biggest fires that most people have ever seen. When they do assist in annihilating the country, they are favoured once again to pop up by the hundreds to dominate, and the cycle starts all over. Mother Nature knows that these plants can get out of hand and cause havoc; that is why she gives us the solution to deal with them.

The flammable invasive natives and weeds are like the pioneers and settlers of the plant world – they can easily travel out of their own country. They can't help but go take over some other ecosystem of native plants. The invasive flammable plants need to be controlled and balanced, otherwise they will destroy the ecosystem altogether. They will take over the native plants that belong there, suppress them, and then try to destroy them, supporting an intense fire that will almost wipe out the native plants and animals altogether. It then gets to the phase of becoming upside-down country, where the roots are sticking in the air and the canopy is on the ground. If we can get on top of these culprits, then it will start to show some positive movement towards managing wildfires and healing the environmental devastation.

Having the wrong vegetation in the country also narrows down the amount of land that can be burnt within the burning window. The fire won't burn at all in many cases because the vegetation is just not going to during the right times. If we had more of the native grass back where it belongs, then we would be able to burn more country to protect it better from wildfires. The native grasses will burn easier and are able to through most times of the burning window. Seeking the long-term transformation of country this way will be a lot of work, but as always, it will get easier in time.

But when such wildfires do occur and wipe everything out, what happens then? People mostly turn their back on the country and think, well, it's all burnt now and that's it. They forget about the poor torched country and turn their backs on it once more, repeating the cycle. The flammable ones shoot again, the parent trees struggle with no canopy, and their scorched leaves fall to suppress the ground floor. If we don't help the country recover, then it will grow to support the next wildfire that will be even worse. Recovery programs need to be put in place to help the country heal. Applying fire and other forms of management the right way will help the country to recover faster. The leaf layer created by the scorched canopy can be burnt in the next season to bring down the dominating unwanted plants. Trying to get control of the balance with the land early is crucial to bring the country back healthy.

Working through country in this condition is dangerous, because of the many dead branches and trees after the fire. People can get killed doing this work, which is why it has to be done with care and safety. There are not many people working on recovering country after wildfires, though there are a few that are now starting to try. Some of them are also getting the fallen logs and trees and laying them sideways along the hill slopes. Trying to position them to catch what is left of the topsoil from being washed away by the heavy rains to come. If we do not do the recovery work, the country will become suppressed for many years and lead to the next phases of wildfire.

Many of the harder storm burn type country can have different problems after the wildfires, like having bare dirt and patches of leaf litter scattered throughout. The country can stay this way for years on end, and burning the leaf litter off has proven effective. Burning the country in this condition is where the emu bobbing comes in. That means walking through the country lighting each patch as you go, getting the layer of leaf off, no matter how thick or thin it is. Bobbing up and down like an emu feeding on country. This is a safe burning application and sometimes it is good to have a number of people involved to help. It is a tedious job for one or two people to do if there is a lot of country in this condition.

Sometimes the country will stay in this condition for many years and still not gain very much fuel loads. Because of this, it will tend to be missed even by hazard reduction burns. They look at country with hardly any fuel loads and think there is no need to burn. Through the Indigenous lens the country needs fire in some way, because there is no vegetation there. No food for the animals, no life within the country. We cannot turn our backs on country like that; we need to look after it too, no matter how big or small the job. Activate the country, awaken it.

There are other invasive native culprits that create different problems within the landscape. The bracken fern can totally take over the country in a way where nothing else will exist. In Tasmania I have visited sites with the Traditional Owners there, where lots of country is being taken over by bracken fern. The country had suffered a severe wildfire and many of the trees were sick or dead, with nothing but bracken covering the country. It had been this way for many years and the bracken was well set in. Nothing in that country can grow again and it was a sad sight to see.

The problem with bracken is that it breaks down lots of old dead fern leaves all the time, which build up beneath the plant. It breaks down to create an interwoven layer that acts like a blanket over the ground. It is almost like a moss or peat layer that sits underneath the loads of dry fern. Healing country in this state will take a long time and if this layer is on country it is not supposed to be; it needs to be done.

A location in Hobart managed by the Traditional Owners had a piece of sandy coastal country that used to have Aboriginal camps in the early days. The site was known to support the Aboriginal people then with food from the land and sea. You could see it was rich country, based on the soil and the trees. The problem today was an intrusive layer of bracken fern that had taken over the area for decades. The bracken fern was at its worst, with the damp mossy blanket layered under all of the dry fern mass.

Digging down into the bracken revealed how it was changing the original sandy ground into a dark soil layer on top. Usually when bracken fern is at this stage it will be wet and moist underneath. The top dry layer shelters it from the sun, allowing it to retain its moisture. If you just burn the top dry layer, the bottom moist layer will not burn, which will result in only bracken fern reshooting. The idea is to burn this state of vegetation layer by layer, over two or even three burns.

The Traditional Owners in Tassie started to conduct the first step of lighting up all of the dead, dry bracken. It was important to light it at a time when it was still sucking a little moisture, to prevent the fire from getting too hot. Just like all invasive natives, they can be very flammable at the wrong times. The fire went well in most places, burning off all of the top layer, which was also helping to dry out the bracken blanket underneath. Once the bottom layer was exposed to the sun, it would then dry out the rest. Making sure you have sunshine following after the burn is a good preparation for this treatment.

After two days or more the final layer was dry and then lit, resulting in a smoky, smouldering fire that slowly burnt away the blanket. The fire went for weeks, but by the end of it all the final layer of bracken was gone. You could see the sandy ground again and we started to walk around, spotting all the different plants returning back to their home. We found orchids, grasses, fruit trees, flowers, and tree sucklings all making their way back onto country. The place felt so much happier and it was so nice to see new life coming through.

Burning the country in layers is good to do for many thick, suppressive weeds and natives. I have conducted layer burns on many occasions and it is good for introduced grasses as well. I have learnt my lessons of not applying the layered burning techniques, and in some cases it's a must. Otherwise the fire can cause too much damage to the country. If you have large amounts of blady grass, or introduced grasses like African lovegrass, you can apply the layered burning styles.

If the bottom layer is dry, then you need to wait for rain to come before you apply the fire. That layer will protect the soil as the top dry grass is burnt away, leaving the same principle of exposing the bottom layer to the sunlight to dry within the next couple of days. Again, burning this way is different to the normal hazard reduction and it takes more time to apply fire this way. But in the end, it will create the best outcome for country and protect the soil as much as possible.

Overall, I am hoping that by now you are seeing just how applying fire to country today is based on a combination of conditions and indicators. It is why we need to train people to be able to manage country and apply fire this way. Whatever the application and fire strategy, it needs to fit the conditions for each place and country. Being able to adapt fire for these diverse conditions is key to healing landscapes this way. To continue to apply the knowledge practically will only improve it into the future and make more sense, culturally and spiritually.

The knowledge of fire the old people handed to me has strengthened since I've applied it to the many challenges within the changed landscape of today. Giving it to the next generations to continue practising the knowledge into the future can only refine it even more. If things don't work out as planned, then we adjust and learn better for next time.

But we know what we need to do – that is to look after the country. We have the knowledge base to work from, so it can only get better as things go on. Not all questions have been answered in this chapter, but I have tried to give a good idea of how to deal with many of the challenges we face with the modern fire management of today. The most important part of healing landscapes with fire is that the country is the boss. The fire practitioners need to be able to see country all the time and make the decision to burn when it is ready. You can't make the decision unless you are reading it from that country and if the right time is there, you must take it.

Chapter 24
Living knowledge

I was in my mid-thirties when I came home from the usual fire adventures and walked into my room to drop the bags. I reached up into the top cupboard to pack stuff when a photo came fluttering down to the floor. It caught my eye, so I reached down to pick it up. It was a photo of me doing a language class with the Elders and schoolkids back in 1994. It looked like I must have been singing one of the Awu-Laya language songs with the children.

It made me smile, fond memories came flowing through from those early days where it all started. I thought about the old people and how important it was to them to be at the school doing language classes. As I looked at the photo, I started to realise something really obvious. To teach the children the knowledge in the schools was what the Elders wanted from day one. I looked happy in the picture and realised that it was the most important work of all. To make a road for the younger generations to follow.

I should have kept on doing that instead of the years trying to break through the hardheads of society. If we are going to make changes to deal with the environmental challenges that lie ahead, then we need to involve the children in the solution. Teach them to take hold of the responsibility of our culture and environment. To learn how we can play our own diverse roles that contribute to the solutions of looking after our planet.

The old people didn't want the young ones to learn this knowledge just to become Indigenous fire practitioners. This knowledge can also help young people to become a teacher at a school, make oils from invasive plants, be a doctor healing people with natural medicines, run a men's or women's group, create inventions, be a farmer planting crops with less water, a lawyer that defends the land and people, or the politician that makes the positive changes for the people and our environment. But most importantly, keep the culture alive and look after the country. Indigenous knowledge is based on holistic thinking which inspires any person's role to be a part of the and solution in caring for community and the environment.

Getting the right fire solutions on country will take a huge shift, involving many good people in many different ways. Everyone is going to be affected if we don't become aware of how we all fit in together to support change. That's why it's important that our kids are learning this at school, that the community are the teachers and the country is the classroom, with children having access to all of the film case studies that are being created by communities. Watching all of the films that are made to teach the process and methods of land management and wellbeing firsthand. Recruiting all of the young people to maintain these responsibilities into the future.

The day that photograph fell to the floor is the day I started to design an online platform called the Living Knowledge Place. It was an attempt to support the Elders' dreams of getting their knowledge into the schools. I didn't want to go back to archiving, but I did want to find a way to get the communities' fire projects into the classroom. A chance came along to put the site together and get the first and only version happening. You could go around certain parts of Australia and access some case studies on Indigenous fire, water, animals, and other cultural projects. It involved non-Indigenous people in some projects, and seemed to be a trial that everyone valued. It went pretty well, but there is a lot of work to do before it is officially working properly for our modern society. I soon learnt that cracking the education nut was just as hard as getting the first fires on country.

But just like lighting the first fires, I went ahead and got help to create the platform that could demonstrate Indigenous teaching methods anyway. It was received very well, and it was a good way to get all the communities involved and trial a shared education site. I trialled creating reading activities and questions from the fire films to inspire kids to read for other subjects. Making the content relevant to culture, our society and our environment is what it is all about. 'Baa, Baa, Black Sheep' is not relevant to us or our environment; we know the song, but we don't know the sheep. We want to learn songs that are crucial to us and relevant to our true identity and surroundings.

The communities were proud to be a part of the site, having their films available for everyone to share. It inspired some of the older generations and families to get out there and get involved. Looking after the land gives you an extra buzz when you know the children are learning about the outcomes. It gives purpose to do the work, knowing that the children are taking notice. It activates culture, pride and understanding when everything moves together. It all seems so straightforward to activate wellbeing, but with no support it is always so hard to get it happening. Building the Living Knowledge Place was to just make it happen – maybe one day it might get a heartbeat and come to life.

Today the groundwork continues and many Indigenous communities are gaining more capacity to get involved. The whole community want to see Aboriginal fire management play a role in looking after the land. Many Aboriginal communities are working together and supporting each other to get the fire programs happening. It seems that people are slowly starting to get it – the broader community are seeing the benefits and sharing the successes. It goes to show that the project model based on the mechanics of traditional knowledge structures works for everyone.

The communities took ownership and made the fire workshops happen, their own motivation sparked the small fire programs in their own country, and the people, both black and white, are supporting each other to make it happen. Indigenous fire programs were resourced from dribs and drabs that the communities and supporting agencies managed to find, but the passion within people made everything possible.

I was proud that I had come all this way with no direct funding from the government. Everything was done from making ends meet along the way and it is amazing how that works out. You don't need lots of money to get things moving; all you need is the right process. The process came from a sustainable knowledge system, and then structure of the work also became sustainable.

It showed that the knowledge was becoming living again, awakened by the country which has been asleep with the people for some time. Keep going and don't give up, regardless of the obstacles in the way. There are plenty of people from community that have given me the strength to pull through. The gratitude and shared passion kept us all going stronger to ensure that the dream of seeing a healthy culture and country will one day be fulfilled.

Throughout 2018 and 2019 the National Indigenous Fire Workshop started moving down to Nowra, hosted by the Yuin nation in New South Wales, and then to Barmah in Victoria, proudly hosted by the Yorta Yorta nation. Hundreds of people attended, realising the need to look after the country. The rural fire and emergency services from both states offered their support and it was so great to see. I was blown away by the support the workshops were gaining right across the board and it was so empowering for all. Little fire workshops hosted by random communities were happening in many places too, lighting up the country and demonstrating the cause. There was so much momentum building up, and burn after burn people became more aware of the need to look after the land. But I could see that it wasn't going to happen before another major time bomb went off.

Throughout the last decade alone I have burnt so much country, in many places and with many different people. But everywhere I go it is the same unmanaged, sick landscapes of excessive fuel loads everywhere, waiting to go off. The drought in the southern parts of Australia started to kick in from 2017 and is still going through 2019. I still kept burning a lot of country throughout this time in Queensland, throughout New South Wales, and a small bit in Victoria. But I could see that a bad fire was going to happen, as nothing was being managed to prevent it. Most of the country was ready for another big fire and it made me feel sorry for every living thing that was immersed within a landscape of neglect.

Even with the drought, the country should have been managed beforehand to best prepare for such conditions. If the country was managed leading up to the drought, we may have had more advantages when dealing with the fire situation. If the country had less flammable vegetation, we could have been burning more country through the drought periods. How can we deal with fire and drought when the country hadn't been managed for many years before? Either way, I kept burning country through this time, to demonstrate that it can at least be done to some level.

The other factor to burning in drought times is to have healthy river systems and waterways. Many of the rivers used to be permanent throughout the country, and many should be able to still flow some water during dry winters. But all the rivers are dry, including all through winter, and many before the drought even started. Fire management becomes harder when the rivers are not healthy and the water has been taken away. It wasn't surprising for me to see most of the drought-stricken trees on country were surrounded by massive corporate industries.

Corporate entities that dam all the catchments and leave the rivers without the blood flow of life, the water. Sorting out our water issues is key to sorting out our fire problems. Not only do you need water to put fire out through the fire hose, but water to flow naturally through the rivers and seep into the land. There is more damage going on with the land than most people think. But I continually hear people blaming the drought alone, giving reasons that exclude all the mismanagement of the land. No doubt the droughts play a harsh role in wildfires, but we could be smarter and better prepared.

By the end of September in 2019, I did my last burn for the year in New South Wales and that was the end of putting any fire to the country. It was just way too dry and by that time the hillsides throughout the country were showing signs of drought-stricken trees in places. The whole country was a tinderbox and I knew that bad fires were going to come. The country wasn't ready to deal with a wildfire as it had no resistance or preparedness at all. I told people that we would come back and try and get more burns happening next year, so only fire planning could happen until then; judging by the way the land was looking, let's hope a wildfire doesn't come and wipe everything out before we can save it.

At the end of the year 2019, the worst expectations happened across many parts of Australia. Wildfires were everywhere and burning to a point that many had never experienced before. Most of the areas that were burning I had visited various times before, and those fuel loads we were restricted from burning were now exploding into fire storms. A fire that was so big that it got the attention of the world, and affected people in cities as much as in the country. The toxic smoke of burnt houses and man-made materials floating through the air and into the lungs of the people. The ashes of the animals and trees mixed within the poisonous haze that left particles of dust on kitchen tables.

The loss of life and property is so heartbreaking, and for some it was their Christmas Day and New Year's Eve. A thousand and more homes destroyed and people fleeing for their lives as evacuation plans turned into military support. These fires raged like the fury of hell, a tragic event recently added to Australia's fire history. Thousands upon thousands of hectares being destroyed as I write this story. Animals are dying to the point where we are heading to the brink of extinction for some. The news stories are going crazy and the debate of climate change hits the front page across the media.

The children march down the street protesting against climate change all over the world in every major city. A schoolgirl speaks at a rally, holding a picture up of her burnt-down house, and tells her devastating story in tears. The response from the right-wing parties on media talk shows is that the children are overreacting about climate change. A group of senior firefighting chiefs stand outside Parliament House to call on the leaders to act on the climate crisis.

Through all this, there's been no acknowledgement by government leadership of looking after the land like the First Nations have done for so long. But my phone is constantly ringing from landholders and communities wanting help. Media articles of Indigenous fire management swoop around the entire world as so many people and places are convinced that we must have positive change. I speak to firefighters and chiefs who want to start cultural burning programs, but they have processes to go through. Schoolteachers are wanting information to share with the children, but they are looking outside of the education system. So many messages of wanting to get community programs happening after the fires, I can't keep up with them. So many communities are ready to start looking after their country and reviving their culture.

For me, 'climate change' has two meanings. There's the climate that has always been changing and humans have been adapting to for thousands of years. The other face of climate change is the man-made situation, where the harmful traits of human action are rapidly contributing. The human damage to the land, mixed with bad land management, has been its own escalating problem that contributes to all of this. There is no separation, it is all part of the one problem and they all need to be dealt with. I am hoping this includes the decline of fossil fuels, improved farming techniques and minimising other contributors to the terrible environmental challenges we face today. Despite the climate changing, it will certainly help to look after the country better along with our precious resources. A leadership oblivious to all this makes it harder to deal with the current problems at hand. We need change right across the board and we have already passed the due date.

The thing with climate change is that it is presented in a way like we can't do anything about it. Just hang our hats on climate change and that is the reason why we are getting all of the fires. Whatever the concerns and views, we need to get away from the debates and just get on with doing something about it. Climate change means the land is telling us something, it is not all doom and gloom. If we look at it the right way, it is an opportunity for change, if we all come to realise it.

It is exciting to see people starting to change, it is just a shame that it takes a massive disaster to make it happen. But it is better late than never; even if it was too late, then we must at least die trying. The massive task of healing the planet will be hard work, but it can be fruitful down the track if we get our backs into it now.

My main concern after these horrible fires have gone out is the government will overlook traditional fire knowledge once more, and give their current services open slather to do hazard reductions and land clearing. Maybe they will also fall back into the line of giving non-indigenous agencies the funds to manage Aboriginal burning programs. I would rather have people out there who know what they are doing, taking into account all the Aboriginal and natural values. The solution to the fires is not to bring back the same old arguments and division within the community. It's time to put together a whole new national approach that this nation has never seen before. It will take everyone being involved and listening to all the expertise that is positive and helps make it happen.

On just one of many occasions in 2017, I was burning country on the coast of central New South Wales. The land was choked up to the max and private houses were in the thick of it. One of the landholders close by was against the burn and was trying to stop it. There were about forty people there and it was a block of land that belonged to the Traditional Owners. They invited the property holder to come and join the group and listen in before he made judgement. Our reading of the land and the story ended with his house sitting among so much fuel it was like a bomb waiting to go off. He was told that if a fire comes this year at the wrong time, all of these houses will be gone.

The man was convinced fully and he began to show signs of warmth and interest. We then put the fire in its right place and away it went, slowly moving its way through the massive fuel load. The Traditional Owners were there to conduct the fire right, though. The flames were low and slow, but only because of the ignition point selected due to the fuel situation. If you apply the fire in the wrong way it could easily go off and burn the trees and all. It was going to take time and patience to burn this country the right way this first-time round, and that's what the participants began to witness. One firefighter character who was gung-ho started shouting out that he could have this fire over in minutes and be out of here. 'Just light the place up and let it go!' and then he laughed out loud. I responded casually that it would burn the whole place down; he agreed and laughed. It was clear that we needed that guy to stay a valued firefighter and keep him away from lighting fires.

The bottom line for me is that we need to work towards a whole other division of fire managers on the land, looking after country in all the ways possible, which includes fire as well as other practices. A skilled team of Indigenous and non-Indigenous people that works in with the entire community, agencies and emergency services to deliver an effective and educational strategy into the future. One that is culturally based and connects to all the benefits for community.

To do that we need to draw on all of our Aboriginal expertise to train people and start upskilling the fire managers of the future. To allow indigenous practitioners from all states to bring together their values and leadership. We need to see three-year training courses of learning out on the country to graduate our Indigenous fire practitioners. We need a chance to at least try – we don't need to hear about the left wing, and the right wing, the continuous separation within our society. We need both wings, so that we can fly.

What we are facing is among the biggest of environmental challenges in modern human history and we need to start dealing with it now. It is not going to be easy and it will take a few years before people will start to see a more effective system take effect. We will still endure bushfires and we will still need the valued fire fighters, but we will see indicators of regeneration to show we are on the right road. It will be a world where we will see smoke and fire more commonly than our current society has ever experienced before, like the early settlers wrote about in their observations on many accounts of seeing Aboriginal people burning in those earlier days.

It will take time for society to adjust – people will have to be supportive and patient to see the benefits down the track. We need to start training the trainers, building the teams, getting people out there on the many different levels. Build from the foundation of Aboriginal knowledge as the practical knowledge base to work from, and adding the Western knowledge to support a stronger solution. Pulling all of our expertises together to create the new wave of a human environmental evolution.

We need new jobs for the young people, to start filling these diverse positions, to take hold of the knowledge and a love for country. There are so many people out there ready to throw down what they are doing to take up the job. I have met so many young people who are willing to throw their weight towards looking after the planet.

It seems that the people of Australia are ready, the agencies are ready to support, and the Aboriginal communities are ready to go. There are Indigenous communities all over Australia, and the world is willing to chip in and give a hand. All that is needed is the resources to match the hard work and community spirit of everyone's efforts and make it become a reality. But who knows, we'll just have to wait and see, I can't really tell how things will go from here. It is really up to the people from here, I just hope positive change happens within my lifetime. All I know is that all the talk is over and now it's time to do something about it.

This book has been a contribution to give the old people a voice and for the land to be heard. I just hope that more people support each other, take up the fight, and do something to save our Aboriginal culture and country for all. To save what all Australians share and to strive towards the greatness we could become. I dedicate my work to the old people of the past and present; it is from them that it passes through all the younger generations, the dreams for the future that are shared. It's for the young people that we seek justice and the triumph is what we will reap in this battle where there is no choice but to win. One thing is for sure, that the truth will never be ignored, and the people will rise to fight the devil in disguise. That is the unknown, that is what we can't see; but to be awakened with all our brothers and sisters of all humanity will set us free.

The most important thing goes back to the younger generations. I hope that they pick up this story and carry on the responsibility. I hope that we are not in this same situation for any amount of time into the future. That the next generations are out on the land once more and not on the streets, protesting and getting hurt. That my own generations see this as a time that we make change for our children. I hope that people have a better understanding of what fire really means and why it is so important.

I sit down quiet tonight. I think about the many destructive fires and what they have done. I think about the days with the old people, and their grandchildren carrying on, the dream to help my own countrymen and women, and the communities that will help each other along, and hope that even after we are all gone, that the next generations will be grateful that the healing has long begun. Fire.

About the author

Victor Steffensen is an Indigenous writer, filmmaker, musician and consultant applying traditional knowledge values in a contemporary context, through workshops and artistic projects. He is a descendant of the Tagalaka people through his mother's connections from the Gulf Country of north Queensland. Much of Victor's work over the past 27 years has been based on the arts and reviving traditional knowledge values – particularly traditional burning – through mentoring and leadership, as well as on-ground training with Aboriginal communities and many non-Indigenous Australians. He is also the co-founder of the National Indigenous Fire Workshops, which have so far been hosted in Queensland, New South Wales and Victoria. Victor has also connected with First Nations communities in California, Canada and the Sámi people of Scandinavia, sharing cultural knowledge practices related to caring for country.

Acknowledgements

I would like to acknowledge my mentors, the late Dr George Musgrave (Snr) and Dr Tommy George (Snr), for believing in me as I believed in them, the journey we started together and vowed to complete. Forever in my heart and will always be proud of what we accomplished together, although it is but a minor contribution to what Aboriginal Australia has to offer our future generations.

I would like to acknowledge my extended families of Dr George Musgrave and Dr Tommy George, who have been there all the way in truth and support. Christine Musgrave, Lewis Musgrave, Dale Musgrave, Eileen George, Rosanne George, Eleanor Musgrave, Destiny Musgrave, all the family and grandchildren, extended families and all of the Laura Aboriginal community (also to acknowledge and respect all the families and mentors we have lost along the way).

Respect to Fred Shepard's family, Tom and Sue Shepard, for your support towards the Musgrave and George families. The story of Fred Shepard hiding those two boys in the mail bags will always be remembered.

In great gratitude to my own family who have always been there in support, including the extended families. I would also like to acknowledge our Aboriginal family connections of the Tagalaka people and full respects to all countrymen and women associated. Thanks to my Uncle Russell Butler for the endorsement of this book.

Special thanks to my good brother Jason De Santolo for being there all the way through, always in support and solidarity. A special thanks to Larissa Behrendt and the Jumbunna Unit of UTS for their valued and continued support.

Beautiful Jacqueline Gothe for your support for so many years and valued friendship, thanks for looking after me. To you and your husband

Michael, and for being so warm and giving me a home in Sydney and becoming like family.

Thanks to James Cook University for acknowledging the Awu-Laya Elders contribution and traditional knowledge through honouring them with their Honorary Doctorates. Thanks to Peta Standley for finishing the PhD and all the help over the years through thick and thin, on behalf of all of us, thank you. Your contribution to help others and the country is respected and much loved by many abroad.

I would like to acknowledge all of the beautiful Aboriginal and Torres Strait Island communities who continue the good fight for the rights of their lands and culture. Big respects to those I have assisted in important initiatives throughout film making, the arts, education and cultural restoration projects, and fire workshops. There are too many to name but they all know who they all are, and all the amazing work we did together and plenty more to come. Respects and thanks to each and every one, as always. Exciting times for community to rise.

A special thanks to Firesticks and all the communities involved that make up such an amazing network of good people from abroad. Thanks to the people who worked hard to keep things together. Jess Wegener, Andry Sculthorpe, Ralph Humes, Amos Atkinson, Brett Ellis, Peta Standley, Kylee Clubb, Sandi Middleton, Rhys Collins, Nova Peris, Noel Webster, Dan Morgan, Barry Hunter, Ruth Gilbert, Jacqueline Gothe, Sian Hromek, Deborah Swan, Darren Chong, Mick Bourke, Leeton Lee, Vera Hong, Craig Bender, and to those who I have missed and to the many people that will be getting involved.

I would like to acknowledge respect to the victims of the bushfires crisis events that have suffered great loss through these tragic events. I also would like to add praise to the fire fighters from all agencies and communities, who have risked their lives and have put in countless efforts to save properties and keeping people safe. Respects to all those who are out there supporting the animals that have also fallen victim to these tragic events.

I would like to acknowledge the emergency services, rural fire agencies in Queensland, NSW and Victoria, local land services, national parks, councils and local schools that have contributed. Special thanks to all of the agencies that have and continue to support the Indigenous fire workshops and assisting Aboriginal communities with their own burning programs. You are all in crucial positions to help make change and is getting stronger as we walk together. So many great things have happened with you all involved and I look forward to sharing in many more.

Special thanks to the masses of non-Indigenous Australians who are in full support of working with Aboriginal people as one. To look after our land and culture for generations to come and for generations to inherit and enjoy. Thanks to those attending workshops and supporting, including making private lands available to train and educate many people while we look after country along the way. This can't happen without you all. Big respects.

Special thanks to those who have endorsed the book – Uncle Russell Butler, Jason De Santolo, Nova Peris, Marcia Langton, Barry Hunter, Jacqueline Gothe, Larissa Behrendt, Uncle David Hudson and Tricia Dearborn.

Special thanks to Hardie Grant for making this book possible and assisting in getting this story out into the world. Thanks to Melissa Kayser and team for your amazing support, it has been a real pleasure working with you all.

Special thanks to Peter McConchie for the photos also acknowledged through the book, *Fire and the Story of Burning Country.*

Thanks to journalist Alasdair McDonald for the use of the photograph of myself at a burn in New South Wales.

I would like to thank everyone that has been involved in some way, shape or form. There are too many amazing people to thank and everyone knows who they are. To all my friends, brothers and sisters who have made me laugh and gave me comfort along the way, truly blessed.